Interactive Notebooks

Grade 8

Credits

Author: Rolanda Williams Baldwin
Content Editors: Elise Craver, Christine Schwab, Angela Triplett

Visit *carsondellosa.com* for correlations to Common Core, state, national, and Canadian provincial standards.

Carson-Dellosa Publishing, LLC
PO Box 35665
Greensboro, NC 27425 USA
carsondellosa.com

978-1-4838-3128-2
01-341157784

Table of Contents

© Carson-Dellosa • CD-104912

What Are Interactive Notebooks?

Interactive notebooks are a unique form of note taking. Teachers guide students through creating pages of notes on new topics. Instead of being in the traditional linear, handwritten format, notes are colorful and spread across the pages. Notes also often include drawings, diagrams, and 3-D elements to make the material understandable and relevant. Students are encouraged to complete their notebook pages in ways that make sense to them. With this personalization, no two pages are exactly the same.

Because of their creative nature, interactive notebooks allow students to be active participants in their own learning. Teachers can easily differentiate pages to address the levels and needs of each learner. The notebooks are arranged sequentially, and students can create tables of contents as they create pages, making it simple for students to use their notebooks for reference throughout the year. The interactive, easily personalized format makes interactive notebooks ideal for engaging students in learning new concepts.

Using interactive notebooks can take as much or as little time as you like. Students will initially take longer to create pages but will get faster as they become familiar with the process of creating pages. You may choose to only create a notebook page as a class at the beginning of each unit, or you may choose to create a new page for each topic within a unit. You can decide what works best for your students and schedule.

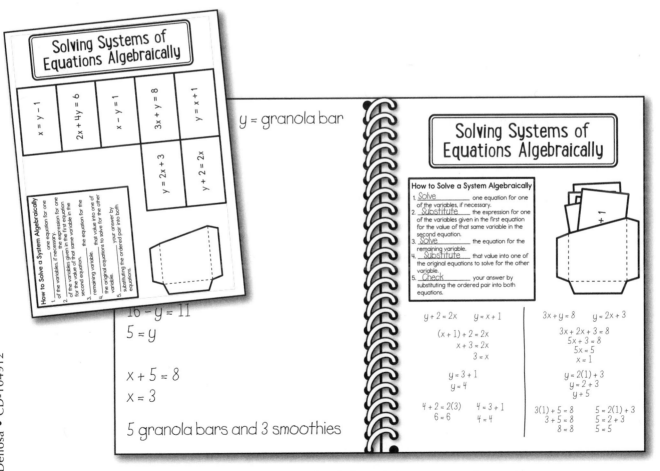

A student's interactive notebook for solving systems of equations

Getting Started

You can start using interactive notebooks at any point in the school year. Use the following guidelines to help you get started in your classroom. (For more specific details, management ideas, and tips, see page 10.)

1. Plan each notebook.

Use the planning template (page 9) to lay out a general plan for the topics you plan to cover in each notebook for the year.

2. Choose a notebook type.

Interactive notebooks are usually either single-subject, spiral-bound notebooks, composition books, or three-ring binders with loose-leaf paper. Each type presents pros and cons. See page 5 for a more in-depth look at each type of notebook.

3. Allow students to personalize their notebooks.

Have students decorate their notebook covers, as well as add their names and subjects. This provides a sense of ownership and emphasizes the personalized nature of the notebooks.

4. Number the pages and create the table of contents.

Have students number the bottom outside corner of each page, front and back. When completing a new page, adding a table of contents entry will be easy. Have students title the first page of each notebook "Table of Contents." Have them leave several blank pages at the front of each notebook for the table of contents. Refer to your general plan for an idea of about how many entries students will be creating.

5. Start creating pages.

Always begin a new page by adding an entry to the table of contents. Create the first notebook pages along with students to model proper format and expectations.

This book contains individual topics for you to introduce. Use the pages in the order that best fits your curriculum. You may also choose to alter the content presented to better match your school's curriculum. The provided lesson plans often do not instruct students to add color. Students should make their own choices about personalizing the content in ways that make sense to them. Encourage students to highlight and color the pages as they desire while creating them.

After introducing topics, you may choose to add more practice pages. Use the reproducibles (pages 78–96) to easily create new notebook pages for practice or to introduce topics not addressed in this book.

Use the grading rubric (page 11) to grade students' interactive notebooks at various points throughout the year. Provide students copies of the rubric to glue into their notebooks and refer to as they create pages.

What Type of Notebook Should I Use?

Spiral Notebook

The pages in this book are formatted for a standard one-subject notebook.

Pros

- Notebook can be folded in half.
- Page size is larger.
- It is inexpensive.
- It often comes with pockets for storing materials.

Cons

- Pages can easily fall out.
- Spirals can snag or become misshapen.
- Page count and size vary widely.
- It is not as durable as a binder.

Tips

- Encase the spiral in duct tape to make it more durable.
- Keep the notebooks in a central place to prevent them from getting damaged in desks.

Composition Notebook

Pros

- Pages don't easily fall out.
- Page size and page count are standard.
- It is inexpensive.

Cons

- Notebook cannot be folded in half.
- Page size is smaller.
- It is not as durable as a binder.

Tips

- Copy pages meant for standard-sized notebooks at 85 or 90 percent. Test to see which works better for your notebook.

Binder with Loose-Leaf Paper

Pros

- Pages can be easily added, moved, or removed.
- Pages can be removed individually for grading.
- You can add full-page printed handouts.
- It has durable covers.

Cons

- Pages can easily fall out.
- Pages aren't durable.
- It is more expensive than a notebook.
- Students can easily misplace or lose pages.
- Larger size makes it more difficult to store.

Tips

- Provide hole reinforcers for damaged pages.

How to Organize an Interactive Notebook

You may organize an interactive notebook in many different ways. You may choose to organize it by unit and work sequentially through the book. Or, you may choose to create different sections that you will revisit and add to throughout the year. Choose the format that works best for your students and subject.

An interactive notebook includes different types of pages in addition to the pages students create. Non-content pages you may want to add include the following:

Title Page

This page is useful for quickly identifying notebooks. It is especially helpful in classrooms that use multiple interactive notebooks for different subjects. Have students write the subject (such as "Math") on the title page of each interactive notebook. They should also include their full names. You may choose to have them include other information such as the teacher's name, classroom number, or class period.

Table of Contents

The table of contents is an integral part of the interactive notebook. It makes referencing previously created pages quick and easy for students. Make sure that students leave several pages at the beginning of each notebook for a table of contents.

Expectations and Grading Rubric

It is helpful for each student to have a copy of the expectations for creating interactive notebook pages. You may choose to include a list of expectations for parents and students to sign, as well as a grading rubric (page 11).

Unit Title Pages

Consider using a single page at the beginning of each section to separate it. Title the page with the unit name. Add a tab (page 78) to the edge of the page to make it easy to flip to the unit. Add a table of contents for only the pages in that unit.

Glossary

Reserve a six-page section at the back of the notebook where students can create a glossary. Draw a line to split in half the front and back of each page, creating 24 sections. Combine Q and R and Y and Z to fit the entire alphabet. Have students add an entry as each new vocabulary word is introduced.

Formatting Student Notebook Pages

The other major consideration for planning an interactive notebook is how to treat the left and right sides of a notebook spread. Interactive journals are usually viewed with the notebook open flat. This creates a left side and a right side. You have several options for how to treat the two sides of the spread.

Traditionally, the right side is used for the teacher-directed part of the lesson, and the left side is used for students to interact with the lesson content. The lessons in this book use this format. However, you may prefer to switch the order for your class so that the teacher-directed learning is on the left and the student input is on the right.

It can also be important to include standards, learning objectives, or essential questions in interactive notebooks. You may choose to write these on the top-left side of each page before completing the teacher-directed page on the right side. You may also choose to have students include the "Introduction" part of each lesson in that same top-left section. This is the *in, through, out* method. Students enter *in* the lesson on the top left of the page, go *through* the lesson on the right page, and exit *out* of the lesson on the bottom left with a reflection activity.

The following chart details different types of items and activities that you could include on each side.

Left Side	Right Side
Student Output	**Teacher-Directed Learning**
• learning objectives	• vocabulary and definitions
• essential questions	• mini-lessons
• I Can statements	• folding activities
• brainstorming	• steps in a process
• making connections	• example problems
• summarizing	• notes
• making conclusions	• diagrams
• practice problems	• graphic organizers
• opinions	• hints and tips
• questions	• big ideas
• mnemonics	
• drawings and diagrams	

Planning for the Year

Making a general plan for interactive notebooks will help with planning, grading, and testing throughout the year. You do not need to plan every single page, but knowing what topics you will cover and in what order can be helpful in many ways.

Use the Interactive Notebook Plan (page 9) to plan your units and topics and where they should be placed in the notebooks. Remember to include enough pages at the beginning for the non-content pages, such as the title page, table of contents, and grading rubric. You may also want to leave a page at the beginning of each unit to place a mini table of contents for just that section.

In addition, when planning new pages, it can be helpful to sketch the pieces you will need to create. Use the following notebook template and notes to plan new pages.

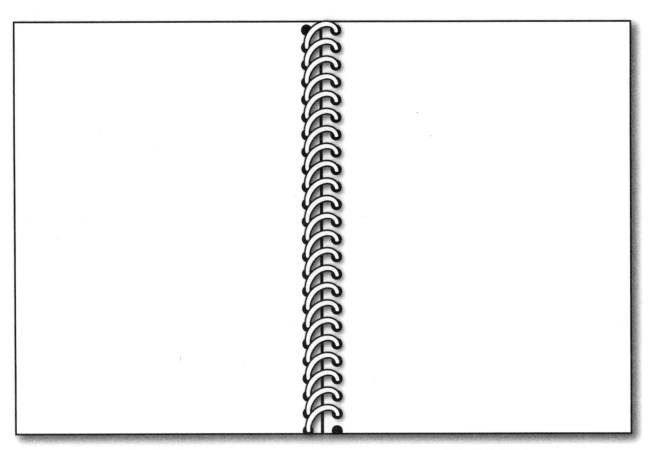

Left Side   **Right Side**

Notes

_____

_____

_____

Interactive Notebook Plan

Page	Topic	Page	Topic
1		51	
2		52	
3		53	
4		54	
5		55	
6		56	
7		57	
8		58	
9		59	
10		60	
11		61	
12		62	
13		63	
14		64	
15		65	
16		66	
17		67	
18		68	
19		69	
20		70	
21		71	
22		72	
23		73	
24		74	
25		75	
26		76	
27		77	
28		78	
29		79	
30		80	
31		81	
32		82	
33		83	
34		84	
35		85	
36		86	
37		87	
38		88	
39		89	
40		90	
41		91	
42		92	
43		93	
44		94	
45		95	
46		96	
47		97	
48		98	
49		99	
50		100	

Managing Interactive Notebooks in the Classroom

Working with Younger Students

- Use your yearly plan to preprogram a table of contents that you can copy and give to students to glue into their notebooks, instead of writing individual entries.

- Have assistants or parent volunteers precut pieces.

- Create glue sponges to make gluing easier. Place large sponges in plastic containers with white glue. The sponges will absorb the glue. Students can wipe the backs of pieces across the sponges to apply the glue with less mess.

Creating Notebook Pages

- For storing loose pieces, add a pocket to the inside back cover. Use the envelope pattern (page 81), an envelope, a jumbo library pocket, or a resealable plastic bag. Or, tape the bottom and side edges of the two last pages of the notebook together to create a large pocket.

- When writing under flaps, have students trace the outline of each flap so that they can visualize the writing boundary.

- Where the dashed line will be hidden on the inside of the fold, have students first fold the piece in the opposite direction so that they can see the dashed line. Then, students should fold the piece back the other way along the same fold line to create the fold in the correct direction.

- To avoid losing pieces, have students keep all of their scraps on their desks until they have finished each page.

- To contain paper scraps and avoid multiple trips to the trash can, provide small groups with small buckets or tubs.

- For students who run out of room, keep full and half sheets available. Students can glue these to the bottom of the pages and fold them up when not in use.

Dealing with Absences

- Create a model notebook for absent students to reference when they return to school.

- Have students cut a second set of pieces as they work on their own pages.

Using the Notebook

- To organize sections of the notebook, provide each student with a sheet of tabs (page 78).

- To easily find the next blank page, either cut off the top-right corner of each page as it is used or attach a long piece of yarn or ribbon to the back cover to be used as a bookmark.

Interactive Notebook Grading Rubric

4

_____ Table of contents is complete.

_____ All notebook pages are included.

_____ All notebook pages are complete.

_____ Notebook pages are neat and organized.

_____ Information is correct.

_____ Pages show personalization, evidence of learning, and original ideas.

3

_____ Table of contents is mostly complete.

_____ One notebook page is missing.

_____ Notebook pages are mostly complete.

_____ Notebook pages are mostly neat and organized.

_____ Information is mostly correct.

_____ Pages show some personalization, evidence of learning, and original ideas.

2

_____ Table of contents is missing a few entries.

_____ A few notebook pages are missing.

_____ A few notebook pages are incomplete.

_____ Notebook pages are somewhat messy and unorganized.

_____ Information has several errors.

_____ Pages show little personalization, evidence of learning, or original ideas.

1

_____ Table of contents is incomplete.

_____ Many notebook pages are missing.

_____ Many notebook pages are incomplete.

_____ Notebook pages are too messy and unorganized to use.

_____ Information is incorrect.

_____ Pages show no personalization, evidence of learning, or original ideas.

Real Number System

Draw a number line labeled from –5 to 5 on the board. Discuss the different types of numbers represented (positive, negative, and zero). Discuss how each type of number is used in a real-world context. Have students give examples of numbers that would fall in between the labeled numbers.

Creating the Notebook Page

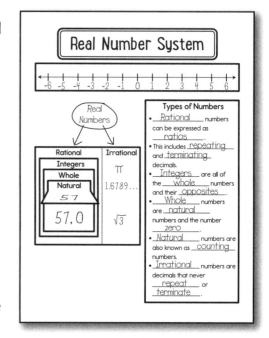

Guide students through the following steps to complete the right-hand page in their notebooks.

1. Add a Table of Contents entry for the Real Number System pages.

2. Cut out the title and glue it to the top of the page.

3. Cut out the number line and label it from –6 to 6. Glue it below the title.

4. Cut out the *Types of Numbers* piece. Glue it below the number line on the right. Complete the explanations. (**Rational** numbers can be expressed as **ratios**. This includes **repeating** and **terminating** decimals. **Integers** are all of the **whole** numbers and their **opposites**. **Whole** numbers are **natural** numbers and the number **zero**. **Natural** numbers are also known as **counting** numbers. **Irrational** numbers are decimals that never **repeat** or **terminate**.)

5. Cut out the *Rational/Irrational* piece. Write *Real Numbers* below the number line on the left. Glue the *Rational/Irrational* piece below it. Draw two arrows to show that real numbers are either rational or irrational.

6. Cut out the *Integers, Whole,* and *Natural* pieces. Apply glue to all three gray glue sections. Stack the pieces to create a stacked flap book (in order: *Rational, Integers, Whole, Natural*).

7. Discuss how if a number is classified as a natural number, it is also considered a whole number, an integer, and a rational number. Use the numbers 57, $-\frac{8}{2}$, $\frac{1}{3}$, π, $\sqrt{3}$, 1.67, 0, –7, 1.6789.... Classify each number by writing it on the appropriate flap(s). Use the number line to better help you understand the real number system and sort the numbers.

Reflect on Learning

To complete the left-hand page, have students think of one more number that could be added to each flap. List each number and the flap it would belong on.

Answer Key
Natural (also whole, integer, rational): 57; Whole (also integer, rational): 0; Integer (also rational): $-\frac{8}{2}$, –7; Rational: $\frac{1}{3}$, 1.67; Irrational: π, $\sqrt{3}$, 1.6789...

Real Number System

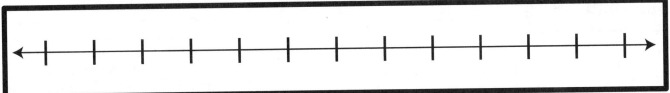

Rational

glue

Irrational

Integers

glue

Natural

Whole

glue

Types of Numbers

- _____ numbers can be expressed as _____ .

- This includes _____ and _____ decimals.

- _____ are all of the _____ numbers and their _____ .

- _____ numbers are _____ numbers and the number _____ .

- _____ numbers are also known as _____ numbers.

- _____ numbers are decimals that never _____ or _____ .

Converting Repeating Decimals to Fractions

Introduction

Have students convert 0.2 to a fraction. (They should rewrite it as $\frac{2}{10}$ and reduce it to $\frac{1}{5}$.) Then, have students convert 0.22 to a fraction. (They should write $\frac{22}{100}$ and reduce it to $\frac{11}{50}$.) Ask students to convert $0.\overline{22}$ to a fraction. Have students share their methods.

Creating the Notebook Page

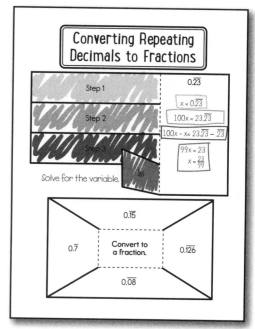

Guide students through the following steps to complete the right-hand page in their notebooks.

1. Add a Table of Contents entry for the Converting Repeating Decimals to Fractions pages.

2. Cut out the title and glue it to the top of the page.

3. Cut out the flap book with the four steps. Cut on the solid lines to create four flaps. Apply glue to the back of the right section and attach it below the title.

4. Under each flap, write a description of the step. (1. Set the repeating decimal equal to a variable. 2. Multiply the variable by the appropriate power of 10. 3. Subtract the original values from each side to remove the repeating decimal. 4. Solve for the variable.)

5. Solve the example problem. If desired, color code the flaps and each step of the process to match.

6. Cut out the *Convert to a fraction* flap book. Cut on the solid lines to create four flaps. Apply glue to the back of the center section and attach it to the bottom of the page.

7. Convert each repeating decimal to a fraction. Write the fraction under the flap.

Reflect on Learning

To complete the left-hand page, have the students evaluate the following expressions:
1. $\frac{2}{3} + 1.\overline{6}$; 2. $0.\overline{18} \times \frac{22}{7}$; 3. $0.\overline{8} - \frac{4}{9}$

Answer Key
Clockwise from top: $\frac{5}{33}$; $\frac{14}{111}$; $\frac{8}{99}$; $\frac{7}{9}$; Reflect: 1. $\frac{7}{3}$; 2. $\frac{2}{11}$; 3. $\frac{4}{9}$

Converting Repeating Decimals to Fractions

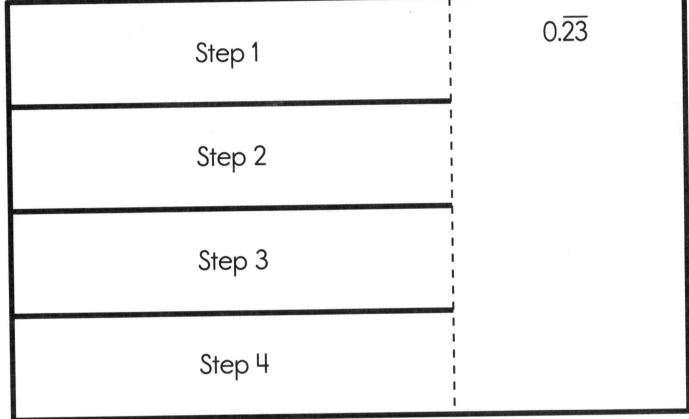

Step 1

Step 2

Step 3

Step 4

$0.\overline{23}$

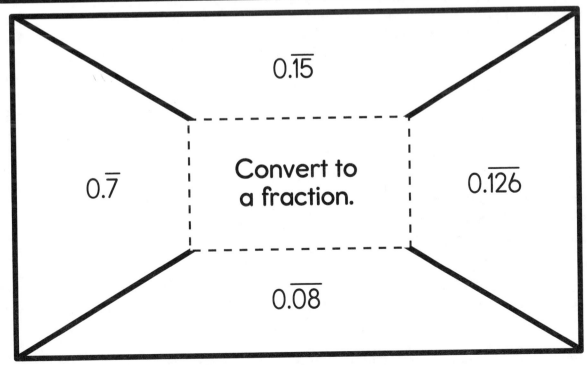

$0.\overline{15}$

$0.\overline{7}$

Convert to a fraction.

$0.\overline{126}$

$0.\overline{08}$

Estimating Square Roots

Introduction

Review the definition of a square root. Have students find the square roots of 25, 81, and 225. Have them discuss with partners how they got the answers (5, 9, and 15). Have students find the square roots of 20, 50, and 150 without a calculator. Have students discuss their answers in small groups. What challenges did they have? How precise were their answers?

Creating the Notebook Page

Guide students through the following steps to complete the right-hand page in their notebooks.

1. Add a Table of Contents entry for the Estimating Square Roots pages.

2. Cut out the title and glue it to the top of the page.

3. Cut out the *Steps to Estimate* flap book and the matching example flap book. Cut on the solid lines to create four flaps on the *Steps to Estimate* flap book. Apply glue to the gray glue section and place the *Steps to Estimate* piece on top to create a stacked eight-flap book. Apply glue to the back of the left section and attach it to the left side of the page below the title.

4. Complete each of the steps. (1. Find the nearest **perfect squares** to the radicand and take the **square roots** of those perfect squares. The square root will be in **between** these two whole numbers. $\sqrt{64} < \sqrt{72} < \sqrt{81}$; $8 < \sqrt{72} < 9$; 2. Find the **difference** between the radicand and the lower perfect square. Find the **difference** between the two perfect squares. $72 - 64 = 8$; $81 - 64 = 17$; 3. Write the differences as a **ratio**. Divide to rewrite the fraction as a **decimal** to the nearest hundredth. $\frac{8}{17}$; $17\overline{)8} = 0.47$; 4. Combine the smaller whole number found in step 1 and the decimal part for an **estimate** of the square root. ($8 + 0.47 = 8.47$) Then, complete the sample problem under the flaps to support the explanation.

5. Cut out the three flaps. Apply glue to the back of the left sections and attach them on the right side of the page.

6. Under each flap, follow the steps from the flap book to estimate the square root.

Reflect on Learning

To complete the left-hand page, have the students solve the following word problem: *Teresa has a string that is $\sqrt{32}$ inches long. Jesse has a string that is $4 \cdot \sqrt{8}$ inches long. Jesse thinks that their strings are of equal length. Is Jesse correct in his thinking? Why or why not?* Students should justify their answers.

Answer Key

$\sqrt{19} \approx 4.3$; $\sqrt{30} \approx 5.45$; $\sqrt{110} \approx 10.48$; Reflect: $\sqrt{32} \approx 5.64$; $4 \cdot \sqrt{8} \approx 4 \cdot 2.80 \approx 11.2$; Jesse has the longer string.

Estimating Square Roots

Steps to Estimate

1. Find the nearest _____ to the radicand and take the _____ of those perfect squares. The square root will be in these two whole numbers.

2. Find the _____ between the radicand and the lower perfect square. Find the _____ between the two perfect squares.

3. Write the differences as a _____ to the nearest hundredth. Divide to rewrite the fraction as a _____.

4. Combine the smaller whole number found in Step 1 and the decimal part for an _____ of the square root.

glue

$$\sqrt{} < \sqrt{72} < \sqrt{}$$
$$\_\_ < \sqrt{72} < \_\_$$

$72 - 64 =$ _____
$81 - 64 =$ _____

$$\frac{8}{17} ; \quad 17\overline{)8}$$

$$\_\_ + 0.\_\_ = \_\_$$

Estimate
$$\sqrt{110}$$
to the nearest hundredth.

Estimate
$$\sqrt{30}$$
to the nearest hundredth.

Estimate
$$\sqrt{19}$$
to the nearest hundredth.

Properties of Integer Exponents

Introduction

Remind students that using exponents is a shorthand way to write repeated multiplication problems. Have students rewrite 2^3 and 2^5 as multiplication problems. Tell students that there are properties that tell us how to operate with expressions that contain exponents.

Creating the Notebook Page

Guide students through the following steps to complete the right-hand page in their notebooks.

1. Add a Table of Contents entry for the Properties of Integer Exponents pages.

2. Cut out the title and glue it to the top of the page.

3. Cut out the *Property* flap book. Cut on the solid lines to create seven flaps. Fold the flaps over on the dashed lines so that the text is inside the flap book. Apply glue to the back of the right section and attach it below the title on the left side of the page.

4. Cut out the property titles. Glue each title on the appropriate flap. (From top: Product of Powers, Power of Product, Quotient of Powers, Power of Quotient, Power of Power, Zero Power, Negative Power)

5. Discuss the proof of each property. Then, complete the rule for each property.
   $(a^m \cdot a^n = a^{m+n};\ (a \cdot b)^m = a^m \cdot b^m;\ \frac{a^m}{a^n} = a^{m-n};\ (\frac{a}{b})^m = \frac{a^m}{b^m};\ (a^m)^n = a^{m \cdot n};\ a^0 = 1;\ a^{-m} = \frac{1}{a^m})$

6. Give an example of each property on the page to the right of the *Proof/Property* flap book.

Properties of Integer Exponents

Property	
Product of Powers	$5^3 \times 5^2 = 5^5$
$(a \times b)^m = a^m \times b^m$	$(4 \times 6)^4 = 4^4 \times 6^4$
Quotient of Powers	$\frac{3^4}{3^2} = 3^2$
Power of Quotient	$(\frac{7}{10})^6 = \frac{7^6}{10^6}$
Power of Power	$(8^2)^4 \times 8^8$
Zero Power	$9^0 = 1$
Negative Power	$3^{-4} = \frac{1}{3^4}$

Reflect on Learning

To complete the left-hand page, have students answer the following problems and tell which property they applied to each:

1. $\frac{4^7}{4^3}$; 2. $(7^3)^5$; 3. $32,150^0$; 4. $8^2 \cdot 8^5$; 5. $\frac{3}{4^2}$; 6. 3^{-4}; 7. $(4 \cdot 3)^5$

Answer Key
Reflect: 1. 4^4, quotient of powers; 2. 7^{15}, power of powers; 3. 1, zero power; 4. 8^7, product of powers; 5. $\frac{3^2}{4^2}$, power of quotient; 6. $\frac{1}{3^4}$, negative power; 7. $4^5 \cdot 3^5$, power of product

Properties of Integer Exponents

		Property
Product of Powers	$2^3 \times 2^4$ $= (2 \times 2 \times 2)(2 \times 2 \times 2 \times 2)$ $= 2^7$	$a^m \times a^n =$ _____
Power of Product	$(2 \times 3)^3$ $= (2 \times 3)(2 \times 3)(2 \times 3)$ $= 2 \times 3 \times 2 \times 3 \times 2 \times 3$ $= 2^3 \times 3^3$	$(a \times b)^m =$ _____
Quotient of Powers	$\dfrac{2^5}{2^3} = \dfrac{2 \times \cancel{2} \times \cancel{2} \times \cancel{2} \times 2}{\cancel{2} \times \cancel{2} \times \cancel{2}}$ $= 2 \times 2 \times 1 \times 1 \times 1 = 2 \times 2$ $= 2^2$	$\dfrac{a^m}{a^n} =$ _____
Power of Quotient	$\left(\dfrac{2}{3}\right)^4 = \dfrac{2}{3} \times \dfrac{2}{3} \times \dfrac{2}{3} \times \dfrac{2}{3}$ $= \dfrac{2 \times 2 \times 2 \times 2}{3 \times 3 \times 3 \times 3} = \dfrac{2^4}{3^4}$	$\left(\dfrac{a}{b}\right)^m =$ _____
Power of Power	$(2^3)^4 = 2^3 \times 2^3 \times 2^3 \times 2^3$ $= (2 \times 2 \times 2)(2 \times 2 \times 2)(2 \times 2 \times 2)(2 \times 2 \times 2)$ $= 2^{12}$	$(a^m)^n =$ _____
Zero Power	$\dfrac{2^3}{2^3} = 2^{3-3} = 2^0$ $\searrow$ $\dfrac{2^3}{2^3} = \dfrac{\cancel{2} \times \cancel{2} \times \cancel{2}}{\cancel{2} \times \cancel{2} \times \cancel{2}} = 1 \times 1 \times 1 = 1 \nearrow$ $= 2^0 = 1$	$a^0 =$ _____
Negative Power	$\dfrac{2^3}{2^5} = 2^{3-5} = 2^{-2}$ $\searrow$ $\dfrac{2^3}{2^5} = \dfrac{\cancel{2} \times \cancel{2} \times \cancel{2}}{2 \times \cancel{2} \times \cancel{2} \times \cancel{2} \times 2} = \dfrac{1 \times 1 \times 1}{2 \times 2} = \dfrac{1}{2^2} \nearrow$ $= 2^{-2} = \dfrac{1}{2^2}$	$a^{-m} =$ _____

Square Roots and Cube Roots

Introduction

Write *14 + 20 = 34* on the board. Ask students what they would do to "undo" this addition problem. Write *3 × 5 = 15*. Ask students how they would "undo" this problem. Finally, write $6^2 = 36$. Have students record how they would "undo" this problem. Students will revisit this at the end of this lesson.

Creating the Notebook Page

Guide students through the following steps to complete the right-hand page in their notebooks.

1. Add a Table of Contents entry for the Square Roots and Cube Roots pages.

2. Cut out the title and glue it to the top of the page.

3. Cut out the flap book. Fold the flaps in on the dashed lines to cover the text. Apply glue to the back of the center section and attach it to the page below the title.

4. Write *square roots* on the top flap and *cube roots* on the bottom flap. Complete the definitions inside of the square root flap. (A **perfect square** is any number that shows the area of a square. The **square root** is the side length.) Write the square and square root equation for each given example. ($3^2 = 9$, $\sqrt{9} = 3$; $2^2 = 4$, $\sqrt{4} = 2$; $1^2 = 1$, $\sqrt{1} = 1$)

5. Complete the definitions inside of the *cube root* flap. (A **perfect cube** is any number that shows the volume of a cube. The **cube root** is the side length). Write the cube and cube root equation for each given example. ($3^3 = 27$, $\sqrt[3]{27} = 3$; $1^3 = 1$, $\sqrt[3]{1} = 1$)

6. Below the flap book, create two reference tables. The first table should contain integer square roots 1–20 and the corresponding perfect squares. The second table should contain integer cube roots 1–10 and the corresponding perfect cubes.

Square Roots and Cube Roots

Square roots

$\sqrt{9} = 3$ $\sqrt{4} = 2$ $\sqrt{1} = 1$

$3^3 = 27$ $1^3 = 1$

$\sqrt[3]{27} = 3$ $\sqrt[3]{1} = 1$

$2^2 = 4$
$\sqrt{4} = 2$

A __perfect__ __cube__ is any number that shows the volume of a cube. The __cube__ __root__ is the side length.

Square Roots

Integer	1	2	3	4	5	6	7	8	9	10	11	12	13	14	15	16	17	18	19	20
Square Root	1	4	9	16	25	36	49	64	81	100	121	144	169	196	225	256	289	324	361	400

Cube Roots

Integer	1	2	3	4	5	6	7	8	9	10
Cube Root	1	8	27	64	125	216	343	512	729	1,000

Reflect on Learning

To complete the left-hand page, have students solve the following equations: $x^3 = 64$; $x^2 = 361$

Answer Key
Reflect: $x = 4$; $x = 19$

Square Roots and Cube Roots

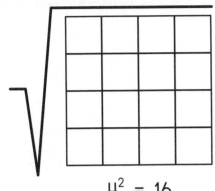

$4^2 = 16$

$\sqrt{16} = 4$

A _____ _____ is any number that shows the area of a square.

The _____ _____ is the side length.

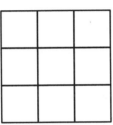

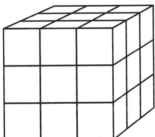

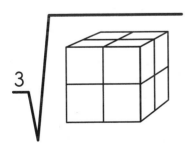

$2^3 = 8$

$\sqrt[3]{8} = 2$

A _____ _____ is any number that shows the volume of a cube.

The _____ _____ is the side length.

Scientific Notation

Have students estimate the distance from Earth to the sun. Write the actual distance on the board (about 92,960,000 miles or 149,604,618.2 km). Then, have students estimate the diameter of an atom. Write the diameter on the board (0.0000000005 meters). Explain that scientific notation is a more concise way to write really large numbers or really small numbers.

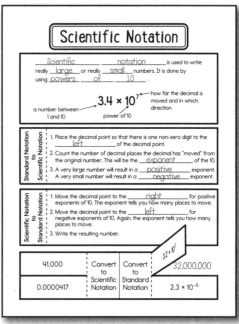

Creating the Notebook Page

Guide students through the following steps to complete the right-hand page in their notebooks.

1. Add a Table of Contents entry for the Scientific Notation pages.

2. Cut out the title and glue it to the top of the page.

3. Cut out the *3.4 × 10⁷* piece. Glue it below the title. Complete the explanation. (**Scientific notation** is used to write really **large** or really **small** numbers. It is done by using **powers of 10**.)

4. Cut out the two flaps. Apply glue to the back of the left sections and attach them below the top piece.

5. Complete the steps on the *Standard Notation to Scientific Notation* flap. (1. Place the decimal point so that there is one non-zero digit to the **left** of the decimal point. 2. Count the number of decimal places the decimal has "moved" from the original number. This will be the **exponent** of the 10. 3. A very large number will result in a **positive** exponent. A very small number will result in a **negative** exponent.) Complete an example under the flap.

6. Complete the steps on the *Scientific Notation to Standard Notation* flap. (1. Move the decimal point to the **right** for positive exponents of 10. The exponent tells you how many places to move. 2. Move the decimal point to the **left** for negative exponents of 10. . . .) Complete an example under the flap.

7. Cut out the flap book. Cut on the solid lines to create four flaps. Apply glue to the back of the center section and attach it to the bottom of the page. Complete the appropriate conversions under each flap.

Reflect on Learning

To complete the left-hand page, have students answer the following question and justify their answers: A typical red blood cell is 3.15×10^{-4} inches wide, while a typical bacterial cell is 0.000039 inches wide. Which is the larger cell?

Scientific Notation

_____ _____ is used to write

really _____ or really _____ numbers. It is done by

using _____ _____ _____ .

$$3.4 \times 10^{7}$$

← how far the decimal is moved and in which direction

a number between →
1 and 10

power of 10

Standard Notation to Scientific Notation

1. Place the decimal point so that there is one non-zero digit to the _____ of the decimal point.

2. Count the number of decimal places the decimal has "moved" from the original number. This will be the _____ of the 10.

3. A very large number will result in a _____ exponent.
   A very small number will result in a _____ exponent.

Scientific Notation to Standard Notation

1. Move the decimal point to the _____ for positive exponents of 10. The exponent tells you how many places to move.

2. Move the decimal point to the _____ for negative exponents of 10. Again, the exponent tells you how many places to move.

3. Write the resulting number.

41,000	Convert to Scientific Notation	Convert to Standard Notation	3.2×10^{7}
0.0000417			2.3×10^{-5}

Operating with Scientific Notation

Introduction

Have students add 3.14 + 6.2. Students should discuss with partners how they added these two numbers. Have students repeat the process for the following problems: 3.14 × 6.2 and 6.2 ÷ 3.14. Students should share the important things to remember when solving each type of problem. Tell students that there are special rules for operating with scientific notation as well.

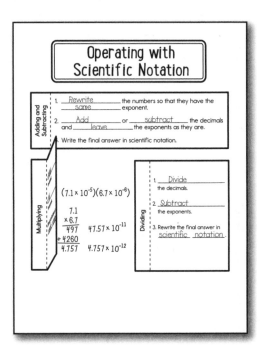

Creating the Notebook Page

Guide students through the following steps to complete the right-hand page in their notebooks.

1. Add a Table of Contents entry for the Operating with Scientific Notation pages.

2. Cut out the title and glue it to the top of the page.

3. Cut out the *Adding and Subtracting* flap. Apply glue to the back of the left section and attach it below the title.

4. Complete the steps. (1. **Rewrite** the numbers so that they have the **same** exponent. 2. **Add** or **subtract** the decimals and **leave** the exponents as they are. 3. Write the final answer in scientific notation.) Lift the flap and complete two examples ($1.08 \times 10^{-3} + 9.3 \times 10^{-3}$ and $9.8 \times 10^4 - 3.48 \times 10^3$).

5. Cut out the *Multiplying* and *Dividing* flaps. Apply glue to back of the left sections and glue them below the *Adding and Subtracting* flap.

6. Complete the steps on the *Multiplying* flap. (1. **Multiply** the decimals. 2. **Add** the exponents. 3. Rewrite the final answer in **scientific notation**.) Lift the flap and complete an example $[(7.1 \times 10^{-5})(6.7 \times 10^{-6})]$.

7. Complete the steps on the *Dividing* flap. (1. **Divide** the decimals. 2. **Subtract** the exponents. 3. Rewrite the final answer in **scientific notation**.) Lift the flap and complete an example ($1.94 \times 10^3 \div 5 \times 10^{-2}$).

Reflect on Learning

To complete the left-hand page, have students use the populations of the United States (3.1×10^8), Canada (3.38×10^7), and Mexico (1.1×10^8) to determine if the population of the United States is more than double the combined populations of Canada and Mexico.

Answer Key
Addition: 1.038×10^{-2}; Subtraction: 9.452×10^4; Multiplication: 4.757×10^{-10}; Division: 3.9×10^4; Reflect: The combined population is 1.438×10^8. The United States population is approximately 2.16 times this combined population.

Operating with Scientific Notation

Adding and Subtracting

1. _____ the numbers so that they have the _____ exponent.

2. _____ or _____ the decimals and _____ the exponents as they are.

3. Write the final answer in scientific notation.

Multiplying

1. _____ the decimals.

2. _____ the exponents.

3. Rewrite the final answer in _____ _____.

Dividing

1. _____ the decimals.

2. _____ the exponents.

3. Rewrite the final answer in _____ _____.

Representing Proportional Relationships

Introduction

Using two volunteers, have one student clap twice for every one time another student snaps his fingers. Tell the student who is snapping his fingers to vary the number of times that he snaps his fingers. Students should record their observations and compare the different ways they recorded the data.

Creating the Notebook Page

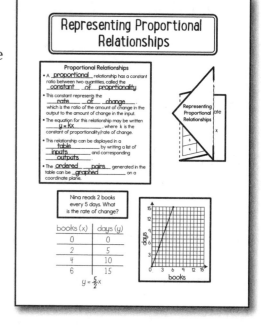

Guide students through the following steps to complete the right-hand page in their notebooks.

1. Add a Table of Contents entry for the Representing Proportional Relationships pages.

2. Cut out the title and glue it to the top of the page.

3. Cut out the *Proportional Relationships* piece and glue it below the title on the left.

4. Complete the explanation. (A **proportional** relationship has a constant ratio between two quantities, called the **constant of proportionality**. This constant represents the **rate of change**, which is the ratio of the amount of change in the output to the amount of change in the input. The equation for this relationship may be written as **y = kx**, where *k* is the constant of proportionality/rate of change. This relationship can be displayed in a **table** by writing a list of **inputs** and corresponding **outputs**. The **ordered pairs** generated in the table can be **graphed** on a coordinate plane.)

5. Cut out the accordion fold. Starting with the arrow end, fold it back and forth on the dashed lines to create an accordion fold with the arrow on top. Apply glue to the back of the last section. Attach it to the right of the *Proportional Relationships* piece.

6. Read the scenario on the arrow and use it to complete the table, graph, and equation ($y = \frac{2}{3}x$) on the remaining sections of the accordion fold.

7. Cut out the graph and the *Nina* piece. Glue them to the bottom of the page, leaving space to solve the problem underneath the text. Complete a table and graph for the scenario. Then, write the rate of change as an equation ($y = \frac{5}{2}x$).

Reflect on Learning

To complete the left-hand page, have students create their own scenarios. They should create the corresponding tables, graphs, equations, and give the constant of proportionality/rate of change.

Representing Proportional Relationships

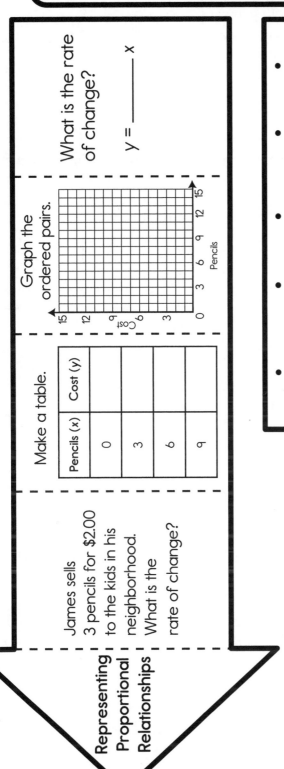

What is the rate of change?

$$y = \underline{\qquad} x$$

Graph the ordered pairs.

Make a table.

Pencils (x)	Cost (y)
0	
3	
6	
9	

James sells 3 pencils for $2.00 to the kids in his neighborhood. What is the rate of change?

Representing Proportional Relationships

Proportional Relationships

- A _____ relationship has a constant ratio between two quantities, called the _____ _____ _____ .

- This constant represents the

  _____ _____ _____ , which is the ratio of the amount of change in the output to the amount of change in the input.

- The equation for this relationship may be written _____ , where k is the constant of proportionality/rate of change.

- This relationship can be displayed in a _____ by writing a list of _____ and corresponding _____ .

- The _____ _____ generated in the table can be _____ on a coordinate plane.

Nina reads 2 books every 5 days. What is the rate of change?

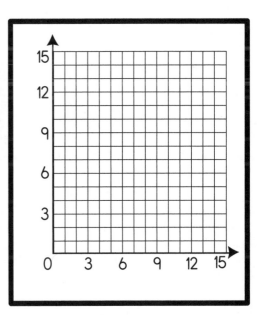

Similar Triangles and Slope

Introduction

Ask students to describe what it means to say that figures are similar. How can one show mathematically whether or not figures are similar? Have students sketch two figures that are similar. Once complete, have students share their similar figures with partners, discussing what makes their figures similar.

Creating the Notebook Page

Guide students through the following steps to complete the right-hand page in their notebooks.

1. Add a Table of Contents entry for the Similar Triangles and Slope pages.

2. Cut out the title and glue it to the top of the page.

3. Cut out the coordinate grid and glue it below the title.

4. Cut out the *Analysis* flap book. Cut on the solid lines to create four flaps. Apply glue to the back of the top section and attach it to the page below the graph.

5. Use the line on the coordinate plane to answer the first question under the flap.

6. Cut out the triangles. Glue each triangle to the graph so that its hypotenuse is aligned with the line graphed on the coordinate grid.

7. Use the triangles and the graph to answer the questions under the remaining flaps.

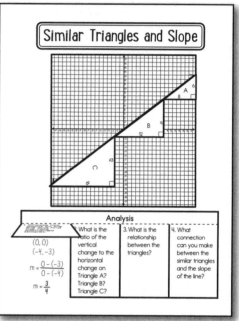

Reflect on Learning

To complete the left-hand page, have the students draw a coordinate plane or provide students with coordinate planes to glue in their notebooks. Given a right triangle with leg lengths of 2 units and 3 units, and another right triangle with leg lengths of 4 units and 6 units, have the students graph a line so that the hypotenuses of the triangles could both lie on the line. Have the students describe the relationship between the triangles. Have the students name another right triangle that could also lie on this line.

Answer Key

1. Ratio will depend on points chosen, but it should reduce to $\frac{3}{4}$. 2. $\frac{6}{8}, \frac{9}{12}, \frac{12}{16}$; 3. The triangles are similar. 4. The rate of change (slope) is the ratio of the vertical change to the horizontal change between points on a line, so each of the ratios of similar right triangles is equal to the rate of change (slope) of the line. Reflect: The triangles are similar. Answers will vary but may include a triangle with leg lengths of 6 units and 9 units.

Similar Triangles and Slope

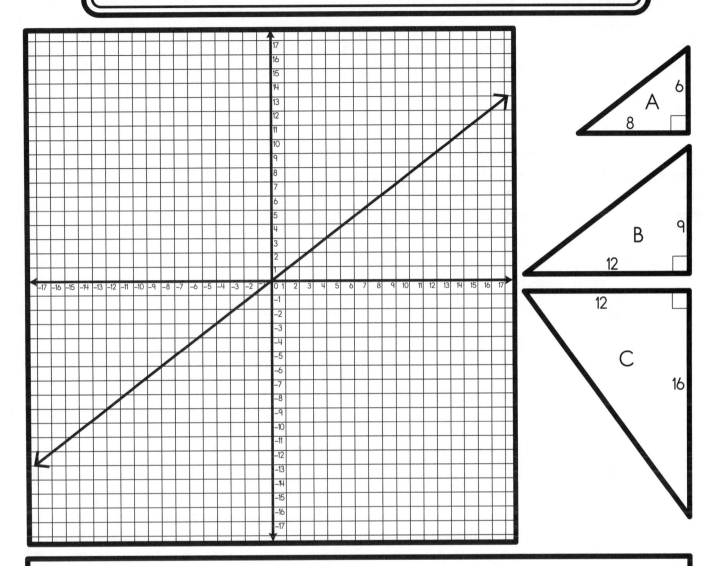

Analysis

1. Choose two points on the line and find the rate of change (slope).

2. What is the ratio of the vertical change to the horizontal change on Triangle A? Triangle B? Triangle C?

3. What is the relationship between the triangles?

4. What connection can you make between the similar triangles and the slope of the line?

Solving Multistep Equations

Introduction

On index cards, write algebraic expressions. Half of the cards should contain expressions that require the use of the distributive property or combining like terms. The other half of the cards should have the matching simplified expressions. Have students find their partners and justify their partnership in writing.

Creating the Notebook Page

Guide students through the following steps to complete the right-hand page in their notebooks.

1. Add a Table of Contents entry for the Solving Multistep Equations pages.

2. Cut out the title and glue it to the top of the page.

3. Cut out the five flaps. Apply glue to the gray glue sections of the steps *1, 2 3, 4* and *5* flaps. Place the flaps on top of each other, aligning the top edges to create a cascading stacked five-flap book with *5* on the bottom and *1* on the top. Glue the stacked flap book below the title on the left side of the page.

4. Cut out the non-numbered equation piece. Apply glue to the remaining gray glue section of the stacked flap book and place the equation piece on top.

5. Complete the steps on the flaps and solve the equation by executing each step on the appropriate flap. (1. Apply the **distributive** property. $6x - 3 - 3 = 4x - 5 - x$; 2. Combine any **like** terms that are on the same side of the equation. $6x - 6 = 3x - 5$; 3. Collect all **variables** on one side of the equation. $3x - 6 = -5$; 4. Collect all **constants** on the opposite side of the variable. $3x = 1$; 5. **Divide** each side by the coefficient. $x = \frac{1}{3}$)

6. Cut out the problem strips. Glue them below or to the right of the stacked flap book, leaving room between each problem for solving. Solve each equation.

Reflect on Learning

To complete the left-hand page, have the students solve the following problem: The Booster Club is selling T-shirts at football games. Vendors must pay $5 for their booths plus 10% of their sales. It costs $8 in materials to make each T-shirt. If the club sells each T-shirt for $10, write and solve an equation to find how many T-shirts they must sell to break even.

Answer Key
1. $x = 2$; 2. $x = \frac{1}{3}$; 3. $x = 3$; 4. $x = 1$; Reflect: $5 + 0.10(10x) + 8x = 10x$; $x = 5$

Solving Multistep Equations

glue

$3(2x - 1) - 3 = 4x - 5 - x$

glue

1. Apply the _____ Property.

glue

2. Combine any _____ terms that are on the same side of the equation.

5. _____ each side by the coefficient.

glue

glue

3. Collect all _____ on one side of the equation.

4. Collect all _____ on the opposite side of the variable.

3. $2(x + 1) = 3x - 1$

2. $2x + 4x = 3x + 1$

4. $2(x + 1) + 2x = 2(x + 2)$

1. $3x + 4x = 14$

Solutions of One-Variable Equations

Introduction

Ask students what it means to have a solution to an equation. Have students substitute 5 for x in the equation $2x + 1 = 11$. Ask the students if 5 is a solution to the equation. Have students justify their answers. Then, have students write their own equations and exchange them with partners. Partners should determine the solutions to the equations.

Creating the Notebook Page

Guide students through the following steps to complete the right-hand page in their notebooks.

1. Add a Table of Contents entry for the Solutions of One-Variable Equations pages.

2. Cut out the title and glue it to the top of the page.

3. Cut out the *Types of Solutions* and *6x + 12* flap books. Cut on the solid lines to create three flaps on each flap book. Apply glue to the gray glue section and place the *Types of Solutions* piece on top to create a stacked six-flap book. Apply glue to the back of the top section and attach it to the page below the title.

4. Under each flap, explain the type of solutions. Use the sample problem to support the explanation.

5. Cut out the *Solve each equation* flap book. Cut on the solid lines to create three flaps. Apply glue to the back of the top section and attach it to the page below the stacked flap book, leaving room to solve the equations below.

6. Use the space on the page below the flap book to solve each equation. Write the type of solution under each flap.

Reflect on Learning

To complete the left-hand page, have the students look at the following equations. Have students decide whether each equation has one solution, no solutions, or infinitely many solutions without solving. Students should explain how they knew the type of solution without solving.
1. $8x + 4 = 4(x - 4)$; 2. $8x + 4 = 4(2x + 1)$; 3. $8x + 4 = 4(2x + 4)$

Answer Key
$8 = 8$, infinitely many solutions; $x = 2$, one solution; $8 = 6$, no solutions; Reflect: 1. one solution; 2. infinitely many solutions; 3. no solutions

32

© Carson-Dellosa • CD-104912

Solutions of One-Variable Equations

Types of Solutions

One Solution	Infinitely Many Solutions	No Solutions
$x = a$	$a = a$	$a = b$

glue

$6x + 12 = 6(2x + 1)$	$6x + 12 = 6(x + 2)$	$6x + 12 = 6(x + 3)$

$$6x + 12 = 12x + 6$$
$$-12x \qquad -12x$$
$$\overline{}$$
$$-6x + 12 = \qquad 6$$
$$ -12 \qquad -12$$
$$\overline{}$$
$$-6x = \qquad -6$$
$$\frac{-6x}{-6} = \frac{-6}{-6}$$
$$x = 1$$

$$6x + 12 = 6x + 12$$
$$-6x \qquad -6x$$
$$\overline{}$$
$$12 = 12$$

True—therefore any number will make the equation true.

$$6x + 12 = 6x + 18$$
$$-6x \qquad -6x$$
$$\overline{}$$
$$12 = 18$$

False—therefore no number can make the equation true.

Solve each equation.

$2x + 8 = \frac{2}{3}(3x + 12)$	$2x + 8 = \frac{2}{3}(6x + 6)$	$2x + 8 = x + 6 + x$

Real-World Systems

Introduction

Tell students that Rosie started a bank account. She started out with an $8 deposit. After a week, she deposited $3 and continued to make the $3 deposit each week. Have students create a table and an equation to represent this scenario. Then, have students compare and discuss their answers in small groups.

Creating the Notebook Page

Guide students through the following steps to complete the right-hand page in their notebooks.

1. Add a Table of Contents entry for the Real-World Systems pages.

2. Cut out the title and glue it to the top of the page.

3. Cut out each flap. Apply glue to the back of the left section of each flap. Attach them to the page below the title.

4. Read the scenario on each flap. Under each flap, create a table to represent the scenario. Then, answer the questions.

Real-World Systems

Scenario 1

Todd and Amani started savings accounts. Todd started with $20 and deposits $5 each week. Amani started with $5 and saves $10 each week. Complete the table. When do Todd and Amani have the same amount in their accounts? Write an equation to represent the total amount in each of their accounts at any given time.

	T	A
0	20	5
1	25	15
2	30	25
3	35	35
4	40	45

They will both have $35 in week 3.

$T = 20 + 5x$
$A = 5 + 10x$

Scenario 2

Todd and Amani started savings accounts. Todd started with $10 and deposits $5 each week. Amani started with $5 and saves $5 each week. Complete the table. Will Todd and Amani ever have the same amount in their accounts? Why or why not? Write an equation to represent the total amount in each of their accounts at any given time.

Scenario 3

Todd and Amani started savings accounts. Todd started with $10 and deposits $4 each week. Amani started with $10 and makes two $2 deposits each week. Complete the table. Will Todd and Amani ever have the same amount in their accounts? Why or why not? Write an equation to represent the total amount in each of their accounts at any given time.

Reflect on Learning

To complete the left-hand page, have students write scenarios about two people who borrow amounts of money from the bank and pay them back weekly. Have students write equations to represent the amount of money each person owes over time and figure out how long it takes for both people to owe the same amount of money.

Answer Key
Scenario 1: They both have $35 at 3 weeks. $T = 20 + 5x$; $A = 5 + 10x$; Scenario 2: They never have the same amount because they start with different amounts and they increase at the same rate. $T = 10 + 5x$; $A = 5 + 5x$; Scenario 3: They always have the same amount because they start with the same amount and they are increasing at the same rate. $T = 10 + 4x$; $A = 10 + 2x + 2x$

Real-World Systems

Scenario 1

Todd and Amani started savings accounts. Todd started with $20 and deposits $5 each week. Amani started with $5 and saves $10 each week. Complete the table. When do Todd and Amani have the same amount in their accounts? Write an equation to represent the total amount in each of their accounts at any given time.

Scenario 2

Todd and Amani started savings accounts. Todd started with $10 and deposits $5 each week. Amani started with $5 and saves $5 each week. Complete the table. Will Todd and Amani ever have the same amount in their accounts? Why or why not? Write an equation to represent the total amount in each of their accounts at any given time.

Scenario 3

Todd and Amani started savings accounts. Todd started with $10 and deposits $4 each week. Amani started with $10 and makes two $2 deposits each week. Complete the table. Will Todd and Amani ever have the same amount in their accounts? Why or why not? Write an equation to represent the total amount in each of their accounts at any given time.

Solving Systems of Equations Graphically

Introduction

Tell students that you have five dimes and nickels in your pocket that total $0.35. How many dimes and nickels are in your pocket? Have students compare their answers with partners. Allow a few groups to share the strategies used.

Creating the Notebook Page

Guide students through the following steps to complete the right-hand page in their notebooks.

1. Add a Table of Contents entry for the Solving Systems of Equations Graphically pages.

2. Cut out the title and glue it to the top of the page.

3. Cut out the *How to Solve* piece. Glue it to the page below the title.

4. Complete the explanations. (A set of two or more **equations** that contain two or more of the same **variables** is a system of equations. The **solution** of a system of equations is a set of **ordered pairs** that make all of the equations in a system true. Since the graph of a function represents all ordered pairs that are solutions to the function equation, if a point lies on the graph of both functions, the point of **intersection** is the solution.)

5. Cut out the shutter fold. Cut on the solid lines to create four flaps on each side. Apply glue to the gray glue section and attach it to the page below the *How to Solve* piece. Fold the flaps in on the dashed lines. Apply glue to the back of the *Solutions* and *Examples* flaps and attach them permanently to the page as column headers.

6. Graph each system on the right flap. Under the left flaps, write if the slope and the *y*-intercept are the same or different. Under the right flaps, explain how the graph system supports the type of solution.

Reflect on Learning

To complete the left-hand page, have students record the three systems of equations below. Students should write how many solutions each system would have without graphing it.

$y = \frac{1}{2}x - 3$ $\qquad$ $y = \frac{1}{2}x - 3$ $\qquad$ $y = \frac{1}{2}x - 3$

$y = \frac{1}{2}(x - 6)$ $\qquad$ $y = -\frac{1}{2}x + 3$ $\qquad$ $y = \frac{1}{2}x + 3$

Answer Key
one solution: (–1, –4); Reflect: one solution; infinitely many solutions; no solution

Solving Systems of Equations Graphically

How to Solve a Using a Graph

- A set of two or more _____ that contain two or more of the same _____ is a system of equations.

- The _____ of a system of equations is a set of _____ _____ that make all of the equations in a system true.

- Since the graph of a function equation represents all ordered pairs that are solutions to the function equation, if a point lies on the graph of both functions, the point of _____ is the solution.

Examples

$y = 2x - 2$
$y = -x - 5$

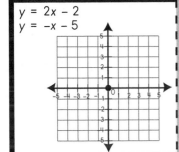

$y = 2x - 4$
$y = 2x + 1$

$y = \frac{1}{3}x + 1$
$y = \frac{1}{3}(x+3)$

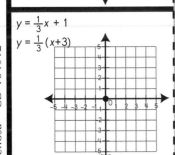

glue

Solutions

One Solution

The graphed lines intersect at exactly one point. There is one ordered pair that satisfies each equation.

No Solution

The graphed lines are parallel and never intersect.

Infinitely Many Solutions

The graphed lines are the same line. They intersect at every point along their length.

Solving Systems of Equations Algebraically

Introduction

Write the system of equations $y = x - 1$ and $y = -\frac{2}{3}x - 2$ on the board. Have students solve it graphically. Have students share their answers with partners and discuss some of the challenges of finding a precise answer. Tell students that trying to solve a system by graphing is not always the best method.

Creating the Notebook Page

Guide students through the following steps to complete the right-hand page in their notebooks.

1. Add a Table of Contents entry for the Solving Systems of Equations Algebraically pages.

2. Cut out the title and glue it to the top of the page.

3. Cut out the *How to Solve* piece and glue it below the title on the left side of the page.

4. Complete the steps. (1. **Solve** one equation for one of the variables, if necessary. 2. **Substitute** the expression for one of the variables given in the first equation for the value of that same variable in the second equation. 3. **Solve** the equation for the remaining variable. 4. **Substitute** that value into one of the original equations to solve for the other variable. 5. **Check** your answer by substituting the ordered pair into both equations.)

5. Cut out the pocket. Apply glue to the back of the tabs and attach it to the page beside the *How to Solve* piece.

6. Cut out the equation cards. Choose two equations. On the bottom of the page, follow the steps to solve the system you have created. Repeat with another pair of equations. Store the cards in the pocket. For extra practice, choose more pairs of equations to solve on another sheet of paper.

Notebook Page Illustration

Solving Systems of Equations Algebraically

How to Solve a System Algebraically

1. __Solve__ one equation for one of the variables, if necessary.
2. __Substitute__ the expression for one of the variables given in the first equation for the value of that same variable in the second equation.
3. __Solve__ the equation for the remaining variable.
4. __Substitute__ that value into one of the original equations to solve for the other variable.
5. __Check__ your answer by substituting the ordered pair into both equations.

$$y + 2 = 2x \qquad y = x + 1$$
$$(x + 1) + 2 = 2x$$
$$x + 3 = 2x$$
$$3 = x$$
$$y = 3 + 1$$
$$y = 4$$
$$4 + 2 = 2(3) \qquad 4 = 3 + 1$$
$$6 = 6 \qquad 4 = 4$$

$$3x + y = 8 \qquad y = 2x + 3$$
$$3x + 2x + 3 = 8$$
$$5x + 3 = 8$$
$$5x = 5$$
$$x = 1$$
$$y = 2(1) + 3$$
$$y = 2 + 3$$
$$y + 5$$
$$3(1) + 5 = 8 \qquad 5 = 2(1) + 3$$
$$3 + 5 = 8 \qquad 5 = 2 + 3$$
$$8 = 8 \qquad 5 = 5$$

Reflect on Learning

To complete the left-hand page, have students solve the following problem: Linda and her friends visit the snack bar at the gym. The snack bar charges $2.00 for a fruit smoothie and $1.00 for a granola bar. The friends buy a total of 8 items for $11.00. Tell how many fruit smoothies and granola bars they bought.

Answer Key
Reflect: 3 fruit smoothies and 5 granola bars

Solving Systems of Equations Algebraically

$x = y - 1$

$2x + 4y = 6$

$x - y = 1$

$3x + y = 8$

$y = x + 1$

$y = 2x + 3$

$y + 2 = 2x$

How to Solve a System Algebraically

1. _____ one equation for one of the variables, if necessary.

2. _____ the expression for one of the variables given in the first equation for the value of that same variable in the second equation.

3. _____ the equation for the remaining variable.

4. _____ that value into one of the original equations to solve for the other variable.

5. _____ your answer by substituting the ordered pair into both equations.

Functions

Introduction

Write the following scenario of cell phone data usage on the board. *A phone plan costs $30 plus $15 for each gigabyte of data used.* Have students calculate the bills for 1 GB, 3 GB, and 5 GB of usage. Have students discuss the scenario with a partner and answer the following question: Could the bills ever be the same amount even if the data usage was different? As a class, discuss and share the results.

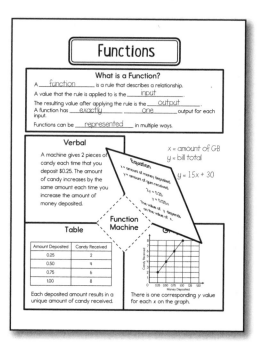

Creating the Notebook Page

Guide students through the following steps to complete the right-hand page in their notebooks.

1. Add a Table of Contents entry for the Functions pages.

2. Cut out the title and glue it to the top of the page.

3. Cut out the *What is a Function?* piece. Glue it to the page below the title.

4. Complete the explanations. (A **function** is a rule that describes a relationship. A value that the rule is applied to is the **input**. The resulting value after applying the rule is the **output**. A function has **exactly one** output for each input. Functions can be **represented** in multiple ways.)

5. Cut out the flap book. Cut on the solid lines to create four flaps. Apply glue to the back of the center section and and attach it to the bottom of the page.

6. Refer back to the scenario given in the introduction. Under each flap, rewrite the scenario using the form represented on the flap.

Reflect on Learning

To complete the left-hand page, have students create scenarios that could be represented by a function. Then, students should represent the scenarios as verbal descriptions, equations, tables, and graphs.

Answer Key
Introduction: $y = 15x + 30$; GB used: 1, 3, 5; Bill Total: 45, 75, 105; Check students' graphs.

Functions

What is a Function?

A _____ is a rule that describes a relationship.

A value that the rule is applied to is the _____.

The resulting value after applying the rule is the _____.
A function has _____ _____ output for each input.

Functions can be _____ in multiple ways.

Verbal

A machine gives 2 pieces of candy each time that you deposit $0.25. The amount of candy increases by the same amount each time you increase the amount of money deposited.

Equation

x = amount of money deposited

y = amount of gum received

$$2y = 0.25$$
$$y = 0.125x$$

The value of y depends on the value of x.

Function Machine

Table

Amount Deposited	Candy Received
0.25	2
0.50	4
0.75	6
1.00	8

Each deposited amount results in a unique amount of candy received.

Graph

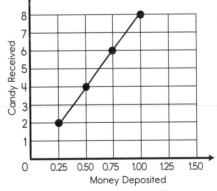

There is one corresponding y value for each x on the graph.

Is It a Function?

Introduction

On index cards, write *hours worked* and fill in various numbers from 4 to 10. Repeat the numbers. Give the cards to students and have them collect their "paychecks." Give students who worked the same number of hours different amounts of pay. Have students compare their pay to that of students who worked the same number of hours. Ask students how it makes them feel to know that they did the same amount of work and didn't get the same pay. Explain that this is dysfunctional–this does not represent a function.

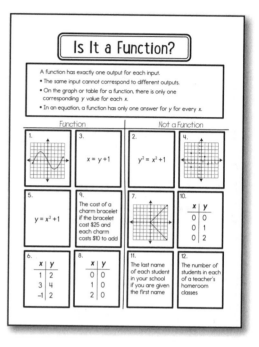

Creating the Notebook Page

Guide students through the following steps to complete the right-hand page in their notebooks.

1. Add a Table of Contents entry for the Is It a Function? pages.

2. Cut out the title and glue it to the top of the page.

3. Cut out the *A function has* piece. Glue it below the title.

4. Discuss the explanation.

5. Draw a T-chart on the page. Label the left column *Function* and the right column *Not a Function*.

6. Cut out the 12 cards. Decide whether or not each card represents a function and glue it in the appropriate column.

Reflect on Learning

To complete the left-hand page, have each student give an example and a non-example of a function for each representation (graph, table, equation, and verbal description).

Answer Key
Function: 1, 3, 5, 6, 8, 9; Not a function: 2, 4, 7, 10, 11, 12

Is It a Function?

A function has exactly one output for each input.

- The same input cannot correspond to different outputs.
- On the graph or table for a function, there is only one corresponding y value for each x.
- In an equation, a function has only one answer for y for every x.

1. 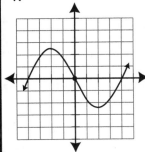	**2.** $y^2 = x^2 + 1$	**3.** $x = y + 1$	**4.** 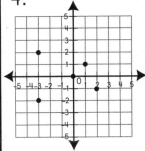
5. $y = x^2 + 1$	**6.** $\begin{array}{c\|c} x & y \\ \hline 1 & 2 \\ 3 & 4 \\ -1 & 2 \end{array}$	**7.** 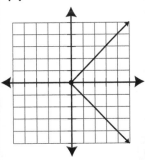	**8.** $\begin{array}{c\|c} x & y \\ \hline 0 & 0 \\ 1 & 0 \\ 2 & 0 \end{array}$
9. The cost of a charm bracelet if the bracelet cost $25 and each charm costs $10 to add	**10.** $\begin{array}{c\|c} x & y \\ \hline 0 & 0 \\ 0 & 1 \\ 0 & 2 \end{array}$	**11.** The last name of each student in your school if you are given the first name	**12.** The number of students in each of a teacher's homeroom classes

Rate of Change in Multiple Representations

Introduction

Write the number pattern *4, 7, 10, 13* on the board. Have students record the pattern. Draw three tally marks on the board. Then, draw six tally marks below it. Continue drawing nine and twelve tally marks below that. Have students record that pattern as well. Explain that the tally marks express the same pattern, even though it is represented differently.

Creating the Notebook Page

Guide students through the following steps to complete the right-hand page in their notebooks.

1. Add a Table of Contents entry for the Rate of Change in Multiple Representations pages.

2. Cut out the title and glue it to the top of the page.

3. Cut out the square piece. Fold each corner on the dashed lines to create four triangular flaps. Apply glue to the back of the center section and attach it to the page below the title, oriented as a diamond.

4. On top of each flap, write *verbal, equation, graph,* and *table* to match the description underneath. Discuss how to find the rate of change with each representation of a function.

5. Cut out the *Find the rate* flap book. Cut on the solid lines to create four flaps. Apply glue to the back of the center section and attach it to the bottom of the page.

6. Under the flaps, find the rate of change for each function.

Reflect on Learning

To complete the left-hand page, write the following problem on the board or provide copies for students to glue in their notebooks. *Jackie's phone bill is represented by the left-hand table and Kendall's phone bill is represented by the right-hand table. Who is paying more per gigabytes of data used? Justify your answer.*

GB used	1	3	5
Bill Total	$45	$75	$105

GB used	1	3	5
Bill Total	$50	$70	$90

Answer Key
Verbal: 0.75; Table: 0.50; Algebraic: 2; Graph: $-\frac{1}{2}$; Reflect: Jackie is paying $15 per GB and Kendall is paying $10 per GB.

Rate of Change in Multiple Representations

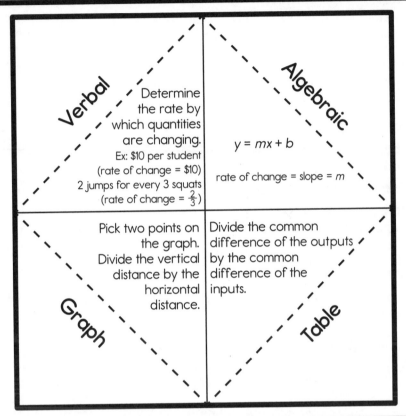

Verbal

Determine the rate by which quantities are changing.
Ex: $10 per student (rate of change = $10)
2 jumps for every 3 squats (rate of change = $\frac{2}{3}$)

Algebraic

$y = mx + b$

rate of change = slope = m

Graph

Pick two points on the graph. Divide the vertical distance by the horizontal distance.

Table

Divide the common difference of the outputs by the common difference of the inputs.

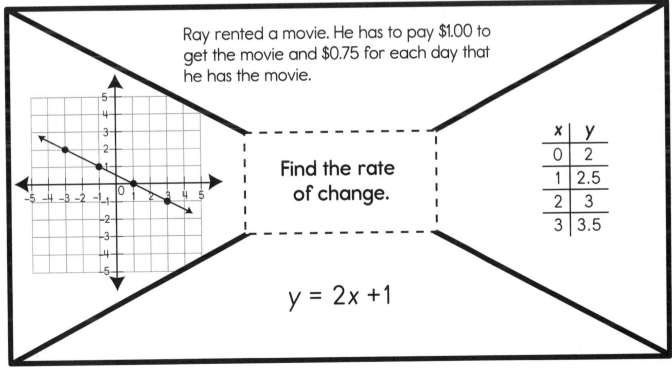

Ray rented a movie. He has to pay $1.00 to get the movie and $0.75 for each day that he has the movie.

Find the rate of change.

$y = 2x + 1$

x	y
0	2
1	2.5
2	3
3	3.5

Comparing Functions in Multiple Representations

Introduction

Write instructions on two index cards. One card should direct a student to clap her hands three times, pause, and then repeat. A second card should direct a student to stomp his foot five times, pause, and then repeat. Give the cards to two students. Have them preform the actions listed on their cards. Ask the other students which of the students is moving more. Explain that even though their actions look different, you can still determine which student is moving more by counting the claps and stomps.

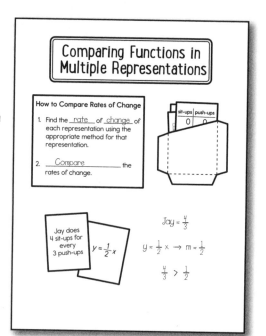

Creating the Notebook Page

Guide students through the following steps to complete the right-hand page in their notebooks.

1. Add a Table of Contents entry for the Comparing Functions in Multiple Representations pages.

2. Cut out the title and glue it to the top of the page.

3. Cut out the *How to Compare* piece. Glue it below the title on the left side of the page.

4. Complete the steps. (1. Find the **rate** of **change** of each representation using the appropriate method for that representation. 2. **Compare** the rates of change.)

5. Cut out the pocket. Apply glue to the back of the tabs and attach it to the page beside the *How to Compare* piece.

6. Cut out the function cards. Choose two functions. On the bottom of the page, follow the steps to solve the functions. Repeat with another pair of functions. Store the cards in the pocket. For extra practice, choose more pairs of functions to solve on another sheet of paper.

Reflect on Learning

To complete the left-hand page, have students solve the following problem: Robert paid $21.00 per T-shirt, including a $15.00 screen-printing fee. Diane's T-shirt costs, which also include the screen-printing fee, are represented by the following table:

# sold	1	3	5
Cost	$20	$30	$40

Who paid the most for each shirt (not including the screen-printing fee)?

Answer Key
Reflect: Diane paid $5 per shirt and Robert paid $6 for each shirt.

Comparing Functions in Multiple Representations

How to Compare Rates of Change

1. Find the _____ of _____ of each representation using the appropriate method for that representation.

2. _____ the rates of change.

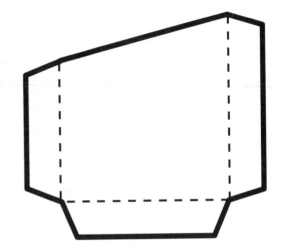

Jay does 4 sit-ups for every 3 push-ups	Kay does 8 sit-ups for every 3 push-ups	sit-ups	push-ups	sit-ups	push-ups
		0	0	0	0
		4	3	5	8
		8	6	10	16
		12	9	15	24
$y = \dfrac{1}{2}x$	$y = \dfrac{4}{3}x$	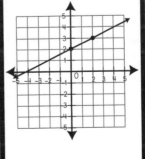		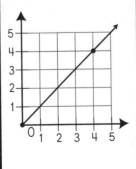	

Linear vs. Nonlinear Functions

Introduction

Write the number pattern *2, 4, 6, 8, 10* on the board. Have students write the answers to the following questions: *What is the pattern? Is the same change occurring between each number?* Write the number pattern *2, 5, 10, 17, 26* on the board. Have students write the answers to the following questions: *How is this different from the last pattern? How is it similar?* Have students discuss their answers with partners.

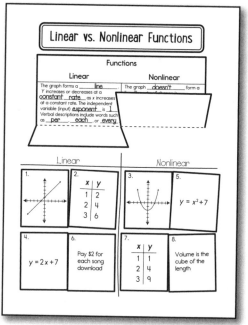

Creating the Notebook Page

Guide students through the following steps to complete the right-hand page in their notebooks.

1. Add a Table of Contents entry for the Linear vs. Nonlinear Functions pages.

2. Cut out the title and glue it to the top of the page.

3. Cut out the *Functions* flap book. Cut on the solid line to create two flaps. Fold on the dashed line to cover the printed sections. Apply glue to the back of the top section and attach it to the page below the title.

4. Complete the explanations under the flaps. (Linear: The graph forms a **line**. *Y* increases or decreases at a **constant rate** as *x* increases at a constant rate. The independent variable (input) **exponent** is **1**. Verbal descriptions include words such as **per**, **each**, or **every**. Nonlinear: The graph **doesn't** form a line. The rate of change is **not constant**. The exponent of the independent variable is **not 1**. Verbal descriptions include words such as **cubed**, **squared**, or **exponentially**.)

5. Draw a T-chart below the flap book. Label it *Linear* and *Nonlinear*.

6. Cut out the function cards. Glue each card in the appropriate column.

Reflect on Learning

To complete the left-hand page, have students give an example of a linear function and a nonlinear function for each representation (graph, table, equation, and verbal description).

Answer Key
Linear: 1, 2, 4, 6; Nonlinear: 3, 5, 7, 8

Linear vs. Nonlinear Functions

Functions

Linear   Nonlinear

Linear

The graph forms a _____ .
Y increases or decreases at a
_____ _____ as x increases
at a constant rate. The independent
variable (input) _____ is _____.
Verbal descriptions include words such
as _____, _____, or _____ .

Nonlinear

The graph _____ form a
line. The rate of change is _____
_____ . The exponent of the
independent variable is _____ _____.
Verbal descriptions include words
such as _____, _____,
or _____ .

1.	2.	3.	4.
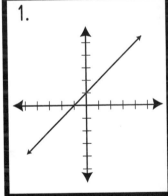	$\begin{array}{c|c} x & y \\ \hline 1 & 2 \\ 2 & 4 \\ 3 & 6 \end{array}$	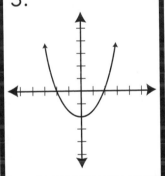	$y = 2x + 7$

5.	6.	7.	8.
$y = x^2 + 7$	Pay $2 for each song download	$\begin{array}{c|c} x & y \\ \hline 1 & 1 \\ 2 & 4 \\ 3 & 9 \end{array}$	Volume is the cube of the length

Anatomy of a Line

Introduction

Have students sketch a coordinate plane. Then, have them plot the point (0, 3). From that point, have them move down 2 units and right 3 units. Have them draw a line to connect the points. Have students plot the point (0, –1). From that point, they should move up 3 units and left 2 units. Students should draw a line to connect those points. Explain that there is an algebraic way to describe each of the lines that they have drawn.

Creating the Notebook Page

Guide students through the following steps to complete the right-hand page in their notebooks.

1. Add a Table of Contents entry for the Anatomy of a Line pages.

2. Cut out the title and glue it to the top of the page.

3. Cut out the two flap books. Cut on the solid lines to create four flaps on the $y = mx + b$ flap book. Apply glue to the gray glue section of the _____ *variable* flap book and place the $y = mx + b$ flap book on top to create a stacked four-flap book. Glue the flap book below the title.

4. Under each flap, complete the explanations (**dependent** variable; **slope**, **rate** of change; **independent** variable; **y-intercept**, where the line **crosses** the y-axis, **initial** value, flat **fee**, **starting** point).

5. Cut out the equation strips.

6. Draw vertical lines down the page between each flap to create four columns. Copy one of the equations below the $y =$ flap. Then, cut the equation strip apart into the four main parts ($y =$, m, x, and b). Glue each part in the correct column. Repeat with the other two equation strips.

Reflect on Learning

To complete the left-hand page, have students write the equations for the lines that they drew in the introduction activity.

Answer Key
Reflect: for the points (0, 3) and (3, 1): $y = -\frac{2}{3}x + 3$; for the points (0, –1) and (–2, 2): $y = -\frac{3}{2}x - 1$

Anatomy of a Line

$$y = \quad m \quad x \quad + b$$

glue

_____ variable

• _____
• _____
of change

_____ variable

• _____
• where the line
  _____ the y-axis
• _____ value
• flat _____
• _____ point

$$y = \frac{2}{3}x + 3$$

$$y = \frac{3}{2}x + \frac{4}{3}$$

$$4 = -y - 3x$$

Interpreting Linear Functions

Introduction

Write $y = 3x + 4$ on the board. Have students find y if x is 4. Then, have them find x if y is 7. Have students insert other values for the variables to test the relationship between the variables.

Creating the Notebook Page

Guide students through the following steps to complete the right-hand page in their notebooks.

1. Add a Table of Contents entry for the Interpreting Linear Functions pages.

2. Cut out the title and glue it to the top of the page.

3. Cut out the flap book on the solid lines, including the short vertical lines on the flaps. Then, fold the left and right flaps toward the center, interlocking them using the small vertical cuts. Apply glue to the back of the center section and attach it to the page below the title.

4. Write b on the left flap and m on the right flap.

5. Open the flaps and complete the explanations. (The slope/rate of change is the **ratio** of the amount of **change** in the output to the change of the input. The y-intercept is a **single** time quantity or **beginning** value.) Pick two points on the *Slope* graph and find the slope using rise/run. Identify the y-intercept on the *y-intercept* graph by circling it and naming the coordinates.

6. Cut out the three accordion folds. Fold on the dashed lines to create three accordion folds. Apply glue to the back of the last section of each. Attach them to the bottom of the page.

7. Discuss how once a linear model is written, values can be substituted for x in order to make predictions. Complete the accordion folds by finding the rate of change, initial value, and linear equation for each given scenario. Use the linear equation to answer the question at the end of the scenario.

Reflect on Learning

To complete the left-hand page, have students use the equations from the accordion folds to answer the following questions: *How long would it take for Jake pay off his loan in full? How long did Katie drive if she only has 2 gallons of gas remaining in her tank? How many songs did the user buy if he spent $13.00?*

Answer Key
2.50/week, –50 (Jake owes $50), $y = 2.50x – 50$, $25 owed (–25); Reflect: –2.5 gallons used, 12 gallons, $y = -2.5x + 12$; 7 gallons remaining; 0.50/song; $5 fee; $y = 0.50x + 5$; $30; 20 weeks; 4 hours; 16 songs

Interpreting Linear Functions

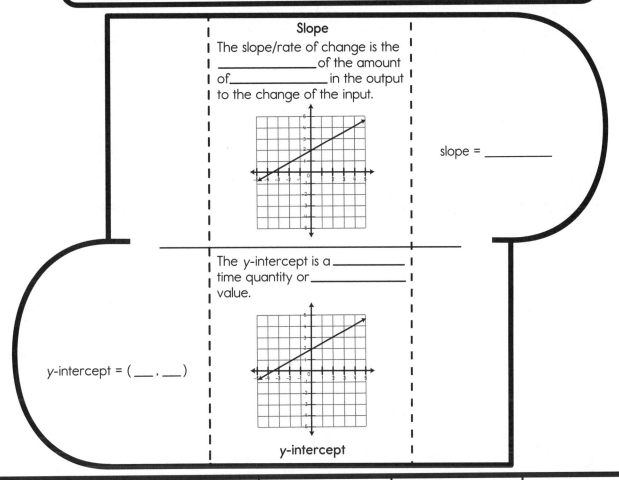

Slope

The slope/rate of change is the _____of the amount of_____in the output to the change of the input.

slope = _____

_____

The y-intercept is a _____ time quantity or_____ value.

y-intercept = (___ , ___)

y-intercept

	Rate of Change	Initial Value	Equation	Final Answer
Jake's mother loans him $50 for concert tickets. He agrees to pay her $2.50 a week until the loan is paid. How much will Jake owe after 10 weeks of payments?				
Katie had 12 gallons of gas in her car when she left her house. She used $2\frac{1}{2}$ gallons of gas each hour that she drove. How many gallons did she have after driving for 2 hours?				
An online music app charges $0.50 per song. How much would it cost to download 50 songs?				

Graph Stories

Students will need a sharpened pencil and a paper clip to complete the spinner activity.

Introduction

Have students think about a roller coaster ride. Have them graph lines that would show their distance from the ground at any given time during the ride. Have students compare their lines with those of their partners. How are their lines similar to their partners'? How are they different?

Creating the Notebook Page

Guide students through the following steps to complete the right-hand page in their notebooks.

1. Add a Table of Contents entry for the Graph Stories pages.

2. Cut out the title and glue it to the top of the page.

3. Cut out the *Determine what* piece. Glue it to the left side of the page under the title.

4. Complete the steps. (Determine what the **x-axis** represents. Determine what the **y-axis** represents. Determine what the **x-intercept** represents. Determine what the **y-intercept** represents. Determine the **rate of change** over each **interval**.)

5. Cut out the *Bike Ride* piece. Glue it to the page to the right of the *Determine what* piece.

6. Using the graph, complete the descriptions of what is happening in each part of the graph. (1. Bike speed **increases**; 2. Bike at a **constant** speed; 3. Bike speed **decreases**; 4. Bike at a **lower** constant speed; 5. Bike speed decreases to a **stop**; 6. Bike is at **rest**; 7. Bike starts **moving** again)

7. Cut out the spinner and graph. Glue them on the bottom of the page, with the spinner on the left.

8. Use a sharpened pencil and a paper clip to spin the spinner. Spin it five times to randomly select sections of the circle. Use the descriptions in the selected sections to draw intervals on the graph.

Reflect on Learning

To complete the left-hand page, have students create their own graph stories. Students should let the *x*-axis represent *time* and the *y*-axis represent *distance from home*. Have students write the scenarios and create the corresponding graphs.

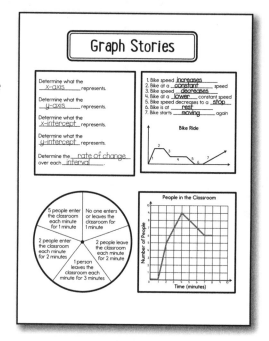

© Carson-Dellosa • CD-104912

Graph Stories

Determine what the _____ represents.

Determine what the _____ represents.

Determine what the _____ represents.

Determine what the _____ represents.

Determine the_____ over each _____.

1. Bike speed _____
2. Bike at a _____ speed
3. Bike speed _____
4. Bike at a _____ constant speed
5. Bike speed decreases to a _____
6. Bike is at _____
7. Bike starts _____ again

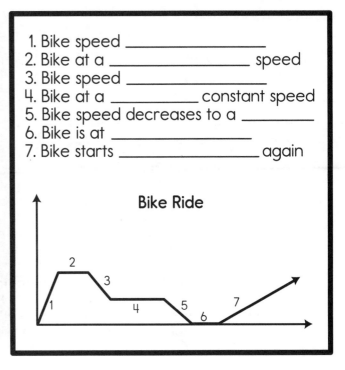

Bike Ride

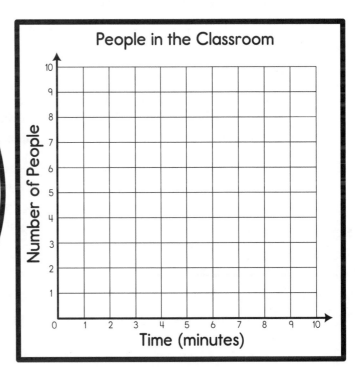

Translations and Reflections on the Coordinate Plane

Introduction

Have students stand beside their desks. Have them take one step forward. Then, ask them to take two steps to the left. Ask them to discuss what has changed (their location). What has not changed (the person)?

Creating the Notebook Page

Guide students through the following steps to complete the right-hand page in their notebooks.

1. Add a Table of Contents entry for the Translations and Reflections on the Coordinate Plane pages.

2. Cut out the title and glue it to the top of the page.

3. Cut out the flap book. Cut on the solid line to create two flaps. Apply glue to the back of the right section and attach it to the page below the title.

4. Cut out the table. Glue it below the flap book. Write the coordinates of each vertex in the table's *Translation and Reflection over x-axis Pre-Image* columns.

5. Cut out the triangle. Place it on top of the triangle on the graph, lining up the edges. Slide the triangle five units to the right and one unit down. This is a translation. Trace the triangle in its new location. Write the coordinates of each vertex in the table's *Image* column.

6. Compare the coordinates. Under the *Translation* flap, write a rule to describe what happens to the coordinates when a figure is translated if j is the number of units moved horizontally and k is the number of units moved vertically.

7. Repeat steps 5 and 6 and flip, or reflect, the triangle across the *x*-axis. Write the rule under the *Reflection* flap. Then, repeat the steps to complete a reflection over the *y*-axis using the reflected triangle as the pre-image. Write the rule under the *Reflection* flap.

Notebook illustration

Translations and Reflections on the Coordinate Plane

Translation
A transformation slides a figure along a straight line. To image has the same size and shape as the pre-image.

$(x, y) = (x + j, y + k)$

Reflection
A transformation flips a figure across a line called the line of reflection. Each point and its images are the same distance from the line of reflection. The image has the same size and shape as the pre-image.

	Translation		Reflection over x-axis		Reflection over y-axis	
	Pre-Image	Image	Pre-Image	Image	Pre-Image	Image
	A(−4, 5)	A. (1, 4)	A(−4, 5)	A. (4, 5)	A(4, 5)	A. (4, −5)
	B(−4, 1)	B. (1, 0)	B(−4, 1)	B. (1, 1)	B(1, 1)	B. (1, −1)
	C(−1, 1)	C. (4, 0)	C(−1, 1)	C. (4, 1)	C(4, 1)	C. (4, −1)

Reflect on Learning

To complete the left-hand page, have students think about video games. Game designers often use a coordinate grid when designing games. Students should explain how reflections and translations could be used to design a video game.

Answer Key
Translation rule: $(x, y) \rightarrow (x + j, y + k)$; Reflection over x-axis rule : $(x, y) \rightarrow (x, -y)$; Reflection over y-axis rule: $(x, y) \rightarrow (-x, y)$; Reflect: Answers will vary but may include translations can be used to move figures throughout a scene. Reflections can be used to change a scene as figures move.

Translations and Reflections on the Coordinate Plane

Translation

A transformation slides a figure along a straight line. The image has the same size and shape as the pre-image.

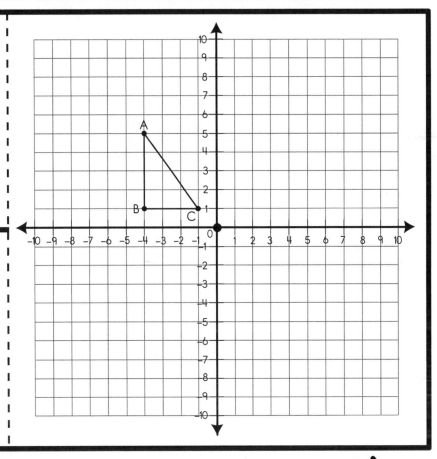

Reflection

A transformation flips a figure across a line called the line of reflection. Each point and its images are the same distance from the line of reflection. The image has the same size and shape as the pre-image.

Translation		Reflection over *x*-axis		Reflection over *y*-axis	
Pre-Image	Image	Pre-Image	Image	Pre-Image	Image

Rotations on the Coordinate Plane

Each student will need a brass paper fastener to complete the right side of the page.

Introduction

Have a student stand in an open area. Place a piece of tape on the floor in front of the student. Have the student rotate around the object, continuously facing the object in the center. Ask students to identify what has changed (the student's location and orientation). Ask students what has not changed (the person).

Creating the Notebook Page

Guide students through the following steps to complete the right-hand page in their notebooks.

1. Add a Table of Contents entry for the Rotations on the Coordinate Plane pages.

2. Cut out the title and glue it to the top of the page.

3. Complete the explanation. (A **rotation** is a transformation that **turns** a figure around a given point called the **center** of **rotation**. The image has the **same** size and shape as the **pre-image**.)

4. Cut out the flap book. Cut on the solid lines to create three flaps. Cut out the triangle spinner. Place the spinner on top of the center dot on the graph. Push a brass paper fastener through the center dots of each piece to attach them. It may be helpful to create the hole in each piece separately first. Apply glue to the back of the right section and attach it to the top of the page. The paper fastener should not go through the page and the triangle should spin freely.

5. Cut out the *90° counterclockwise* table. Glue it below the flap book.

6. Write the coordinates of each vertex in the table's *Pre-Image* columns. Rotate the triangle 90° counterclockwise, using the dashed line in quadrant II as a guide. Mark the triangle's new vertices and connect them to form the triangle. Label the interior of the triangle with the rotation. Write the coordinates of the new triangle in the *Image* column. Compare the coordinates. Under the *90°* flap, write a rule to describe the change to the coordinates.

7. Repeat step 6 for the *180°* and *270° counterclockwise* rotations, respectively.

Reflect on Learning

To complete the left-hand page, have students use triple Venn diagrams to compare and contrast translations, reflections, and rotations.

Answer Key
90° counterclockwise: $(x, y) \rightarrow (-x, y)$; 180°: $(x, y) \rightarrow (-x, -y)$; 270° counterclockwise: $(x, y) \rightarrow (x, -y)$

Rotations on the Coordinate Plane

A __rotation__ is a transformation that __turns__ a figure around a given point called the __center__ of __rotation__. The image has the __same__ size and shape as the __pre-image__.

90° counterclockwise		180° counterclockwise		270° counterclockwise	
Pre-Image	Image	Pre-Image	Image	Pre-Image	Image
A(2, 2)	A. (−2, 2)	A(2, 2)	A. (−2, −2)	A(2, 2)	A. (2, −2)
B(6, 2)	B. (−2, 6)	B(6, 2)	B. (−2, −6)	B(6, 2)	B. (2, −6)
C(6, 6)	C. (−6, 6)	C(6, 6)	C. (−6, −6)	C(6, 6)	C. (6, −6)

Rotations on the Coordinate Plane

A _____ is a transformation that _____ a figure around a given point called the _____ of _____ . The image has the _____ size and shape as the _____ .

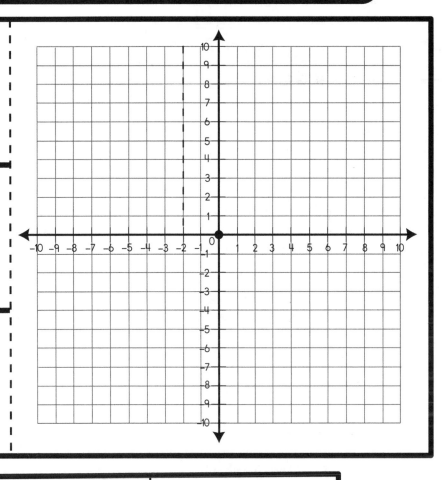

90° counterclockwise
(270° clockwise)

180°

270° counterclockwise
(90° clockwise)

90° counterclockwise		180° counterclockwise		270° counterclockwise	
Pre-Image	Image	Pre-Image	Image	Pre-Image	Image

Dilations on the Coordinate Plane

Introduction

Give each student or small group a wide rubber band. Have them draw stick figures or balloons on them. Ask them to watch what happens when they stretch the rubber bands slowly and then relax them. As a group, discuss how the figure changes size but continues to resemble the original figure.

Creating the Notebook Page

Guide students through the following steps to complete the right-hand page in their notebooks.

1. Add a Table of Contents entry for the Dilations on the Coordinate Plane pages.

2. Cut out the title and glue it to the top of the page.

3. Cut out the flap book. Cut on the solid line to create two flaps. Apply glue to the back of the left section and attach it below the title.

4. Complete the explanation. (A dilation is a transformation that **enlarges** or **shrinks** a figure from a given point. It creates a **similar** figure. A dilation is created by multiplying a **scale factor** by each coordinate.)

5. Then, complete the explanations on the flaps. (If the scale factor is **greater** than 1, then the image is **larger** than the pre-image. If the scale factor is **less** than 1 but greater than 0, then the image is **smaller** than the pre-image.) Write two examples of a scale factor that would result in a larger image under the top flap. Write two examples of a scale factor that would result in a smaller image under the bottom flap.

6. Cut out the two flaps. Apply glue to the gray glue section and place the *Try It!* flap on top to create a stacked two-flap book. Glue the stacked flap book to the bottom of the page.

7. On each flap, write the coordinates of the triangle in the *Pre-Image* column. Multiply each coordinate by the scale factor to generate the coordinates of the image. Draw the new figures on the coordinate plane.

Reflect on Learning

To complete the left-hand page, have students think about the effect of the scale factor. Students should describe how a scale factor of 1 would affect the pre-image. Then, have students describe real-world situations where a scale factor other than 1 would be useful.

Answer Key
Table 1: (0, 4), (−4, −4), (4, −4); Table 2: (0, 1), (−1, −1), (1, −1); Reflect: A scale factor of 1 would cause the image to stay the same size.

Dilations on the Coordinate Plane

A dilation is a transformation that _____ or _____ a figure from a given point. It creates a _____ figure. A dilation is created by multiplying a _____ _____ by each coordinate.

If the scale factor is _____ than 1, then the image is _____ than the pre-image.

If the scale factor is _____ than 1 but greater than 0, then the image is _____ than the pre-image.

Try It

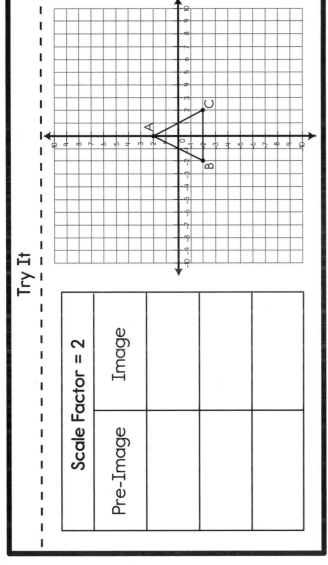

Scale Factor = 2		
Pre-Image		
Image		

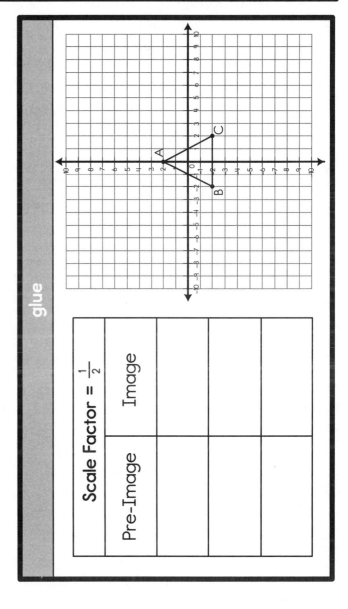

Scale Factor = $\frac{1}{2}$		
Pre-Image		
Image		

glue

Triangle Angle Theorems

Introduction

Review supplementary angles with students. Have students work in pairs to draw two supplementary angles. Have each set of partners verify their angles with another pair of partners. As a class, draw a set of three supplementary angles.

Creating the Notebook Page

Guide students through the following steps to complete the right-hand page in their notebooks.

1. Add a Table of Contents entry for the Triangle Angle Theorems pages.

2. Cut out the title and glue it to the top of the page.

3. Cut out triangle 1. Tear off each "corner," making sure that each corner fully includes one angle of the triangle.

4. Draw a point on the page under the title and to the left, leaving some space above it. Glue each piece to the page around the point so that no corners overlap and no gaps are between the pieces.

5. Cut out the *Triangle Sum Theorem* flap. Apply glue to the back of the top section of the flap and attach it below the rearranged triangle on the left.

6. Answer the questions and complete the examples under the flap.

7. Cut out triangle 2. Glue it to the page beside the rearranged triangle. Label the interior angles *1–3*. Extend the base of the triangle and label the exterior angle, opposite angle 3, as angle *4*.

8. Cut out the *Exterior Angle Theorem* flap. Apply glue to the back of the top section and attach it to the right of the *Triangle Sum Theorem* piece.

9. Answer the questions and complete the examples under the flap.

Reflect on Learning

To complete the left-hand page, have students sketch a triangle and draw all of its exterior angles. Then, have students write the number of exterior angles that the triangle has at each vertex. Students should assign angle measures to one of the exterior angles and one of the remote interior angles and use the theorems to calculate the measures of the remaining interior angles.

Answer Key

Triangle Sum Theorem: 1. Angles form a straight line; 2. $180°$; 3. the sum of angles from the triangle add up to $180°$; 4. $180°$; 5. $25°$;
Exterior Angle Theorem: 2. straight line, $180°$; 3. $m\angle 1 + m\angle 2 + m\angle 3 = + m\angle 3 + m\angle 4$; 4. $m\angle 1 + m\angle 2 = m\angle 4$;
6. $2y + 6 = 70°$, $y + 8 = 40°$

Triangle Angle Theorems

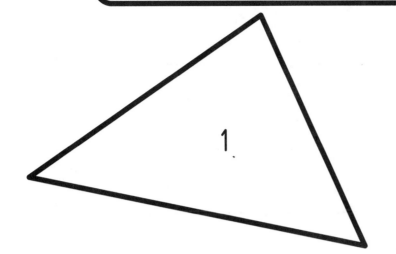

1.

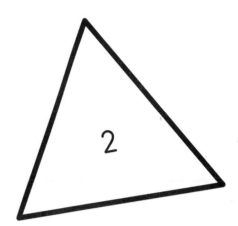

2

Triangle Sum Theorem

1. How did the angles fit together around a point?

2. What is the measure of a straight angle?

3. What is the relationship, in words, between the measure of the angles in the triangle?

4. The Triangle Sum Theorem states that for $\triangle ABC$, $m\angle A + m\angle B + m\angle C =$ _____.

5. Find the missing angle measure.

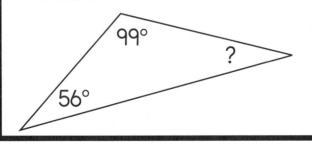

Exterior Angle Theorem

1. Restate the Triangle Sum Theorem.

2. What do angles 3 and 4 form? What is the sum of the measures of angles 3 and 4?

3. You can set the sum of the interior angles equal to the sum of the angles 3 and 4 since they both equal 180°. Write the resulting equation.

4. Simplify the equation in step 3. What is the resulting equation?

5. The Exterior Angle Theorem states that the measure of an exterior angle is equal to the sum of its remote interior angles.

6. Find the measure of each interior angle.

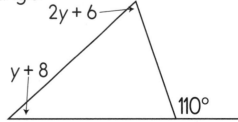

The Pythagorean Theorem

Show students several squares drawn on grid paper. Have students describe how they would find the area of each of the squares. Then, have students practice finding the area of each square provided.

Creating the Notebook Page

The Pythagorean Theorem

Area of square on leg a	Area of square on leg b	Area of square on hypotenuse
16	9	25
36	64	100
25	144	169
81	144	225
a^2	b^2	c^2

Guide students through the following steps to complete the right-hand page in their notebooks.

1. Add a Table of Contents entry for The Pythagorean Theorem pages.

2. Cut out the title and glue it to the top of the page.

3. Cut out the three squares.

4. Calculate the area of each square and write it on the square. Arrange the squares so that one side of each square forms the leg of a right triangle. Glue the squares below the title to secure the right triangle on the page.

5. Label the legs and the hypotenuse of the right triangle.

6. Cut out the *Area of* flap. Apply glue to the back of the top section and attach it to the page below the triangle.

7. Complete the first row of the table using the triangle that you formed. Complete the remaining rows with the following: 36, 64, 100; 25, 144, 169; and 81, 144, 225.

8. Based on the data in the table, describe under the flap how the areas of the squares that form the legs relate to the area of the square that forms the hypotenuse. Assign the legs the variables a and b, and assign the variable c to the hypotenuse. Write an equation that relates the legs and hypotenuse of right triangles ($a^2 + b^2 = c^2$).

Reflect on Learning

To complete the left-hand page, have students think about what the lesson just proved. The sum of the squares of the legs of a right triangle equals the square of the hypotenuse. Have students use the following measures for the sides of right triangles to prove that if $a^2 + b^2 = c^2$, then the triangle is a right triangle: (5, 12, 13) (7, 24, 25) and (8, 15, 17).

Answer Key
The sum of the areas of the squares on the legs in a right triangle is equivalent to the square area of the hypotenuse. $a^2 + b^2 = c^2$;
Reflect: $5^2 + 12^2 = 13^2$, 25 + 144 = 169, 169 = 169; $7^2 + 24^2 = 25^2$, 49 + 576 = 625, 625 = 625; $8^2 + 15^2 = 17^2$, 64 + 225 = 289, 289 = 289

The Pythagorean Theorem

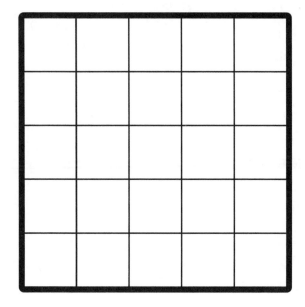

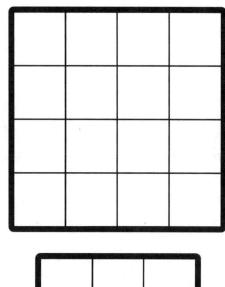

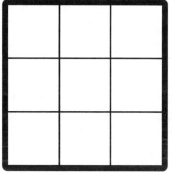

Area of square on leg a	Area of square on leg b	Area of square on hypotenuse
a^2	b^2	c^2

Applying the Pythagorean Theorem

Introduction

Have students solve the following equations: $x^2 = 25$ and $x^2 = 100$. Then, have students estimate the following to the nearest tenth: $\sqrt{30}$ and $\sqrt{90}$. Explain that students can solve real-world problems by using the Pythagorean Theorem to solve for the missing variable using square roots.

Creating the Notebook Page

Guide students through the following steps to complete the right-hand page in their notebooks.

1. Add a Table of Contents entry for the Applying the Pythagorean Theorem pages.

2. Cut out the title and glue it to the top of the page.

3. Cut out the *Given any two measures* piece. Glue it under the title.

4. Complete the piece by filling in the blanks. [Given any two measures (*a*, *b*, or *c*) of a right triangle, use the **Pythagorean Theorem** to find the length of the missing side. 1. **Substitute** known values into the formula. 2. **Simplify.** 3. Use the properties of equality to get the **squared term** by itself. 4. Take the **square root** of both sides.]

5. Cut out the flap book. Cut on the solid lines to create three flaps. Apply glue to the back of the left section and attach it to the bottom of the page.

6. Read each example problem. Label each blank triangle with the information from the problem. Under the flap, solve the problem.

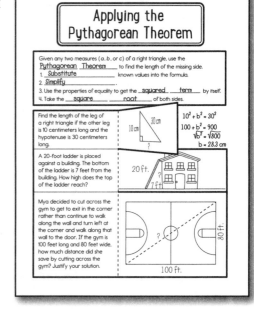

Reflect on Learning

To complete the left-hand page, have students think about the process of solving for a missing side of a right triangle. Have students answer the question, "When given the length of one side and the hypotenuse, does it matter whether you substitute the length of the leg for *a* or for *b*?" Students should write their answers and explain their reasoning.

Answer Key
28.3 cm; 18.7 ft. 51.9 ft.; Reflect: It doesn't matter if you use *a* or *b* for the leg because of the commutative property of addition.

Applying the Pythagorean Theorem

Given any two measures (a, b, or c) of a right triangle, use the
_____ _____ to find the length of the missing side.

1. _____ known values into the formula.

2. _____.

3. Use the properties of equality to get the _____ _____ by itself.

4. Take the _____ _____ of both sides.

Find the length of the leg of a right triangle if the other leg is 10 centimeters long and the hypotenuse is 30 centimeters long.

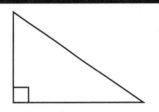

A 20-foot ladder is placed against a building. The bottom of the ladder is 7 feet from the building. How high does the top of the ladder reach?

Mya decided to cut across the gym to get to exit in the corner rather than continue to walk along the wall and turn left at the corner and walk along that wall to the door. If the gym is 100 feet long and 80 feet wide, how much distance did she save by cutting across the gym? Justify your solution.

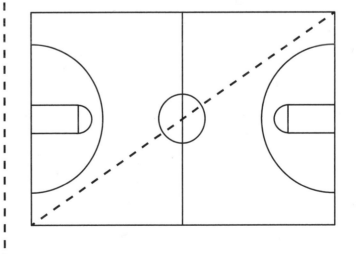

Distance on the Coordinate Plane

Introduction

Have students draw a diagonal line on a coordinate plane. Then, have students calculate the length of the line, showing their work and writing their final answers. Ask students to share the methods they used. Have students discuss the challenges they faced when trying to figure out the distance of the diagonal lines.

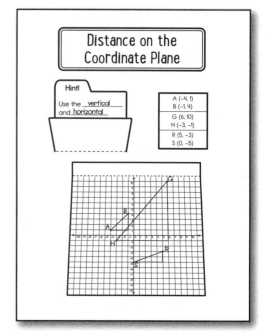

Creating the Notebook Page

Guide students through the following steps to complete the right-hand page in their notebooks.

1. Add a Table of Contents entry for the Distance on the Coordinate Plane pages.

2. Cut out the title and glue it to the top of the page.

3. Cut out the *Hint!* mini file folder. Fold it in half on the dashed line so that the text is inside the folder. Apply glue to the back and attach it below the title on the left side of the page so the open edge of the folder is on top.

4. Open the folder and complete the hints. (Use the **vertical** and **horizontal** distances between the two points as the legs and the length of the **diagonal** as the hypotenuse.)

5. Cut out the coordinate piece and glue it beside the folder.

6. Cut out the graph flap. Apply glue to the back of the top section and attach it to the bottom of the page.

7. Plot the sets of points from the coordinates piece on the graph and find the distance between the two points using the hint. Use the space under the flap to show your work. Round the answer to the nearest tenth.

Reflect on Learning

To complete the left-hand page, have students find the perimeter of a quadrilateral with coordinates at (–5, –1), (–2, –1), (–4, –4), and (–1, –3). Students should round answers to the nearest tenth.

Answer Key
4.2 units; 14.2 units; 5.4 units; Reflect: 11.6 units

Distance on the
Coordinate Plane

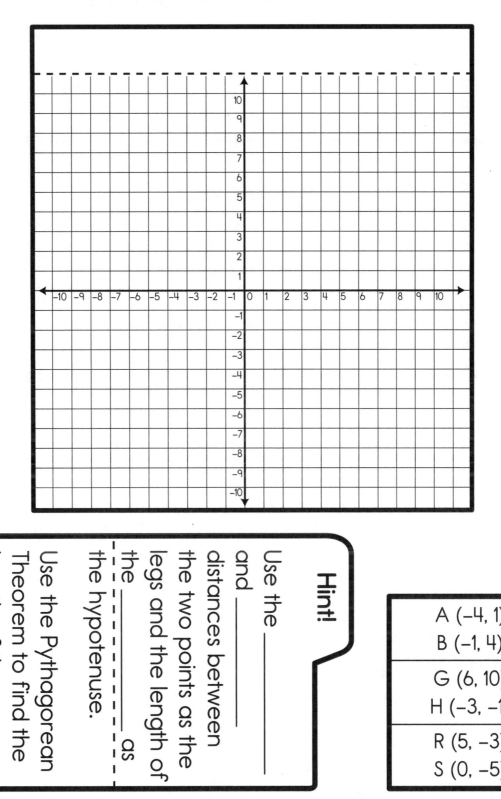

Hint!

Use the _____
and _____
distances between
the two points as the
legs and the length of
the _____ as
the hypotenuse.

Use the Pythagorean
Theorem to find the
length of the
hypotenuse (c).

| A (–4, 1) |
| B (–1, 4) |
| G (6, 10) |
| H (–3, –1) |
| R (5, –3) |
| S (0, –5) |

Volume of Cylinders, Cones, and Spheres

Introduction

Review the area of a circle. What does the area represent? What is the radius in relation to a circle? What is the diameter in relation to the radius? Have students find the area of a circle with the radius of 5 centimeters. Repeat with a circle with a diameter of 14 meters.

Creating the Notebook Page

Guide students through the following steps to complete the right-hand page in their notebooks.

1. Add a Table of Contents entry for the Volume of Cylinders, Cones, and Spheres pages.

2. Cut out the title and glue it to the top of the page.

3. Cut out the *Cylinder*, *Cone*, and *Sphere* accordion folds. Starting with the gray glue section, fold the pieces back and forth on the dashed lines to create an accordion fold with the title on top. Apply glue to the gray glue sections and attach them to the page below the title.

4. Complete the cylinder accordion fold. (Base: **circle**; Area of Base: πr^2; Height: h; Volume: $V = \pi r^2 h$) Complete an example ($r = 2$, $h = 3$) on the page to the right of the accordion fold.

5. Complete the cone accordion fold. (Base: **circle** Area of Base: πr^2; Height: h; Volume: $V = \frac{1}{3} \pi r^2 h$) Complete an example ($r = 2$, $h = 3$) on the page to the right of the accordion fold.

6. Complete the sphere accordion fold. (Related Shape: **circle**; Area of Related Shape: πr^2; Height: r; Volume: $V = \frac{4}{3} \pi r^3$) Complete an example ($r = 2$) on the page to the right of the accordion fold.

7. Cut out the *How much toothpaste* piece and glue it to the bottom of the page.

8. Solve the problem using the volume formulas.

Reflect on Learning

To complete the left-hand page, have students solve the following problem: Julie has a spherical water balloon. She needs it to hold between 80 and 90 cubic inches of water. What is a possible radius for the ball?

Answer Key
cylinder: 37.68 units³; cone: 12.57 units³; sphere: 33.51 units³; 20.94 cm³; Reflect: around 2.7 inches

Volume of Cylinders, Cones, and Spheres

glue	glue	glue
Volume	Volume	Volume
Height	Height	Height
Area of Base	Area of Base	Area of Related Shape
Base	Base	Related Shape
Cylinder	Cone	Sphere

Scatter Plots

Introduction

Have students think about the relationship between the price of a car and the year it was made. Have them discuss with partners whether overall prices of cars have increased or decreased over time. Then, have students sketch a graph to show what they discussed with their partners. Finally, have students think about missed assignments and the numeric value of their scores. Students can discuss with partners what happens to a grade as the number of missed assignments increases. Have students sketch a graph to show what they discussed with their partners. Explain that often data points don't create a straight line, but they still show relationships. Scatter plots are a useful way to show these relationships.

Creating the Notebook Page

Guide students through the following steps to complete the right-hand page in their notebooks.

1. Add a Table of Contents entry for the Scatter Plots pages.

2. Cut out the title and glue it to the top of the page.

3. Complete the title by filling in the blanks. (a graph with points plotted to show the **relationship** between **two sets** of data)

4. Cut out the *Distance to School* flap. Apply glue to the back of the left section and attach it below the title.

5. Plot each ordered pair from the table on the graph. Under the flaps, write your observations about the graph.

6. Cut out the *Types of Association* flap book. Cut on the solid lines to create three flaps. Apply glue to the back of the top section and attach it to the page below the graph.

7. Discuss the three types of association. Write example scenarios under each flap, such as the time spent studying and the grades on a test (positive association); the time driven and the amount of gas in the car (negative association); or letters in a name and the number of siblings (no association).

Reflect on Learning

To complete the left-hand page, have students think about real-world relationships. Ask students to write their own examples of scenarios with positive association, negative association, and no association.

Scatter Plots

a graph with points plotted to show the _____
between _____ _____ of data

Distance to School (miles)	Length of Commute (minutes)
1	5
3	5
5	10
6	12
2	4
3	6
7	15

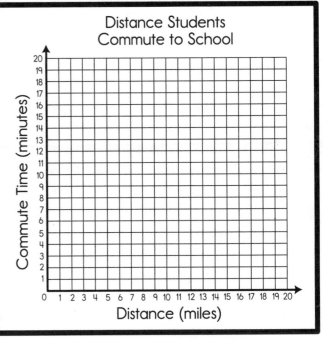

Distance Students Commute to School

Types of Association

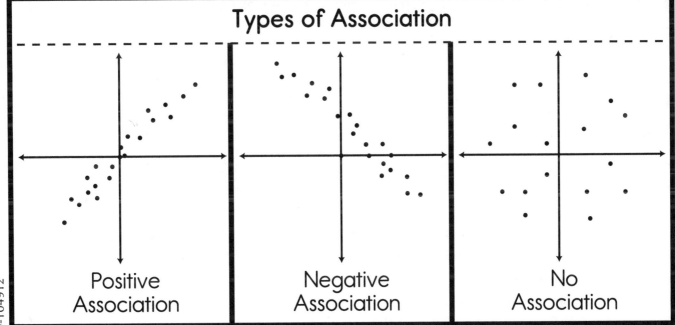

Positive Association

Negative Association

No Association

Linear Models

Introduction

Display a data table with the following data on the board:

Distance Run (miles)	4	1	3	5	4	2
Time (minutes)	38	7	26	55	45	25

Ask students to predict how long it would take this person to run six miles. Write all of the predictions on the board. Explain that a linear model can produce a more exact prediction.

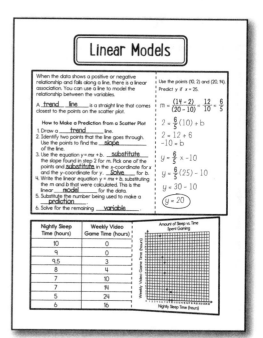

Creating the Notebook Page

Guide students through the following steps to complete the right-hand page in their notebooks.

1. Add a Table of Contents entry for the Linear Models pages.

2. Cut out the title and glue it to the top of the page.

3. Cut out the *When the data shows* flap. Apply glue to the back of the left section and glue it below the title.

4. Complete the left side of the flap book with steps for making predictions based on a scatter plot. (A **trend line** is a straight line that comes closest to the points on the scatter plot. 1. Draw a **trend** line. 2. Identify two points that the line goes through. Use the points to find the **slope** of the line. 3. Use the equation $y = mx + b$. **Substitute** the slope found in step 2 for m. Pick one of the points and **substitute** in the x-coordinate for x and the y-coordinate for y. **Solve** for b. 4. Write the linear equation $y = mx + b$, substituting the m and b that were calculated. This is the linear **model** for the data. 5. Substitute the number being used to make a **prediction**. 6. Solve for the remaining **variable**.

5. Follow the steps to complete the example on the flap. Use the additional space under the flap if needed.

6. Cut out the graph flap. Apply glue to the back of the left section and attach it below the *When the data shows* flap. Plot the points using the data table. Under the flap, make a prediction about how long a student would play video games if he slept 8.5 hours a night.

Reflect on Learning

To complete the left-hand page, have students think about the trend line that was just found. Students should describe the meaning of the slope and the y-intercept in this situation.

Answer Key

Sample trend line: $y = -4.8x + 45$; A student who sleeps 8.5 hours a night probably plays 4.2 hours of video games per week.

Reflect: The slope means that one hour of sleep will be lost for every 4.2 hours of video games played weekly. The y-intercept means that if a student plays 45 hours of video games, then he will get no sleep.

Linear Models

When the data shows a positive or negative relationship and falls along a line, there is a linear association. You can use a line to model the relationship between the variables.

A _____ _____ is a straight line that comes closest to the points on the scatter plot.

How to Make a Prediction from a Scatter Plot

1. Draw a _____ line.
2. Identify two points that the line goes through. Use the points to find the _____ of the line.
3. Use the equation $y = mx + b$. _____ the slope found in step 2 for m. Pick one of the points and _____ in the x-coordinate for x and the y-coordinate for y. _____ for b.
4. Write the linear equation $y = mx + b$, substituting the m and b that were calculated. This is the linear _____ for the data.
5. Substitute the number being used to make a _____.
6. Solve for the remaining _____.

Use the points (10, 2) and (20, 14).

Predict y if $x = 25$.

Nightly Sleep Time (hours)	Weekly Video Game Time (hours)
10	0
9	0
9.5	3
8	4
7	10
7	14
5	24
6	16

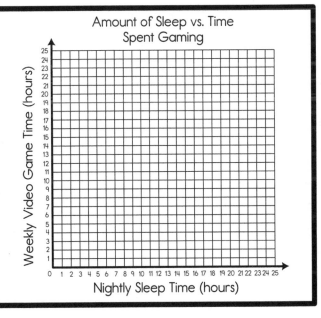

Amount of Sleep vs. Time Spent Gaming

Two-Way Tables

Introduction

Tell students that sometimes two sets of data are best displayed in a table rather than a scatter plot. Take a quick poll of the class. Ask students if they have siblings. Record the data in two tables. In the first table, record all responses together. In the second table, record male and female responses separately. For example, tally male students that have siblings and males that do not have siblings. As a class, compare and contrast the two types of tables.

Creating the Notebook Page

Guide students through the following steps to complete the right-hand page in their notebooks.

1. Add a Table of Contents entry for the Two-Way Tables pages.

2. Cut out the title and glue it to the top of the page.

3. Complete the title. (A two-way table shows data that pertains to two different **categories**.)

4. Cut out the *Fifty eighth-grade students* piece. Glue it to the page below the title.

5. Explain how to read the table. Use the data to complete the table.

6. Cut out the *Analyze the Data* flap book. Cut on the solid lines to create four flaps. Apply glue to the back of the top section and attach it to the page below the data table.

7. Review the procedure for calculating percentages. Answer each question under the flap.

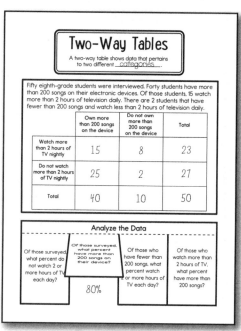

Reflect on Learning

To complete the left-hand page, have students create surveys for their classmates. Have them conduct the surveys and create two-way tables to display the data. Then, have students write two questions that can be used to analyze the data.

Answer Key
From left to right: 54%; 80%; 80%; 65%

© Carson-Dellosa • CD-104912

Two-Way Tables

A two-way table shows data that pertains to two different _____.

Fifty eighth-grade students were interviewed. Forty students have more than 200 songs on their electronic devices. Of those students, 15 watch more than 2 hours of television daily. There are 2 students that have fewer than 200 songs and watch less than 2 hours of television daily.

	Own more than 200 songs on the device	Do not own more than 200 songs on the device	Total
Watch more than 2 hours of TV nightly			
Do not watch more than 2 hours of TV nightly			
Total			

Analyze the Data

Of those surveyed, what percent do not watch 2 or more hours of TV each day?

Of those surveyed, what percent have more than 200 songs on their device?

Of those who have fewer than 200 songs, what percent watch 2 or more hours of TV each day?

Of those who watch more than 2 hours of TV, what percent have more than 200 songs?

Tabs

Cut out each tab and label it. Apply glue to the back of each tab and align it on the outside edge of the page with only the label section showing beyond the edge. Then, fold each tab to seal the page inside.

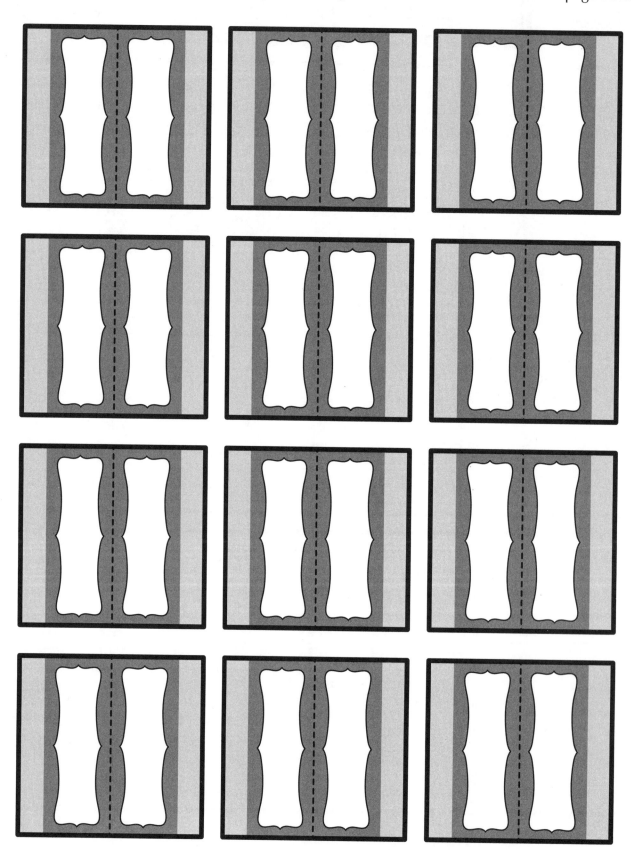

Cut out the KWL chart and cut on the solid lines to create three separate flaps. Apply glue to the back of the Topic section to attach the chart to a notebook page.

Topic: _____

What I

Know

What I

Wonder

What I

Learned

Library Pocket

Cut out the library pocket on the solid lines. Fold in the side tabs and apply glue to them before folding up the front of the pocket. Apply glue to the back of the pocket to attach it to a notebook page.

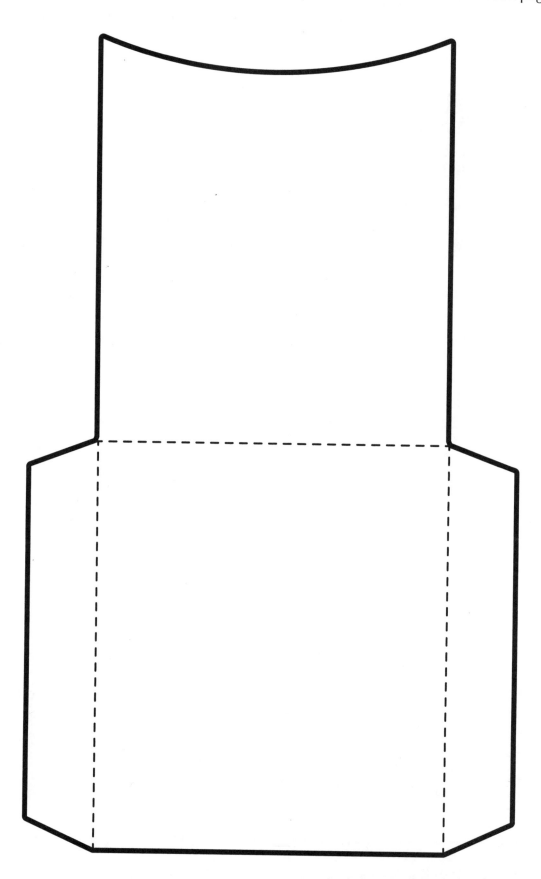

Cut out the envelope on the solid lines. Fold in the side tabs and apply glue to them before folding up the rectangular front of the envelope. Fold down the triangular flap to close the envelope. Apply glue to the back of the envelope to attach it to a notebook page.

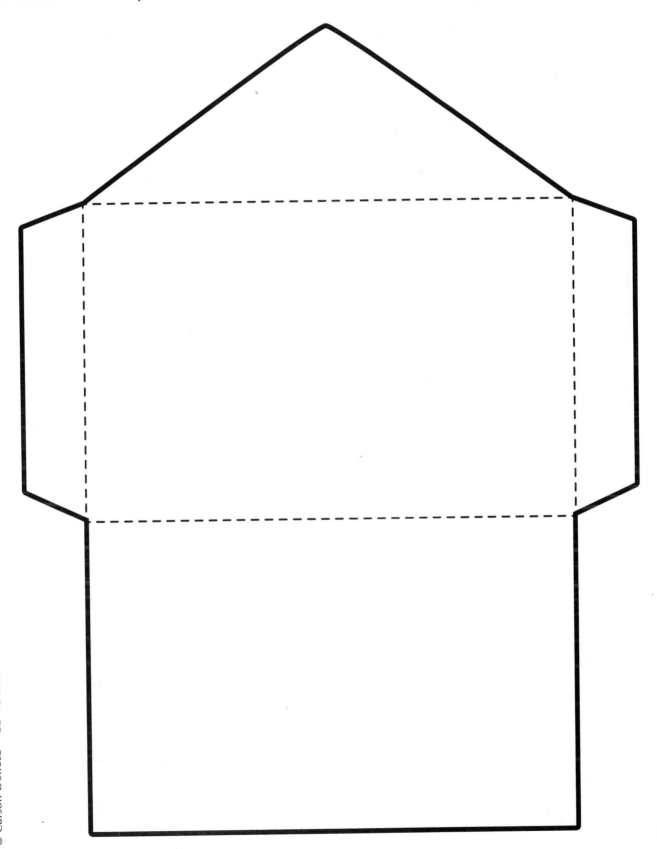

Pocket and Cards

Cut out the pocket on the solid lines. Fold over the front of the pocket. Then, apply glue to the tabs and fold them around the back of the pocket. Apply glue to the back of the pocket to attach it to a notebook page. Cut out the cards and store them in the envelope.

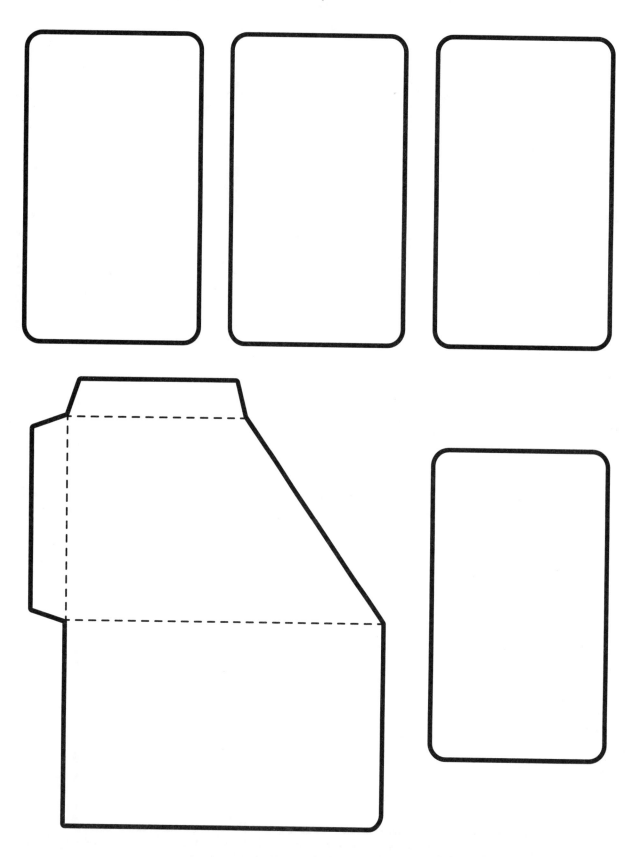

Six-Flap Shutter Fold

Cut out the shutter fold around the outside border. Then, cut on the solid lines to create six flaps. Fold the flaps toward the center. Apply glue to the back of the shutter fold to attach it to a notebook page.

If desired, this template can be modified to create a four-flap shutter fold by cutting off the bottom row. You can also create two three-flap books by cutting it in half down the center line.

Eight-Flap Shutter Fold

Cut out the shutter fold around the outside border. Then, cut on the solid lines to create eight flaps. Fold the flaps toward the center. Apply glue to the back of the shutter fold to attach it to a notebook page.

If desired, this template can be modified to create two four-flap shutter folds by cutting off the bottom two rows. You can also create two four-flap books by cutting it in half down the center line.

Flap Book—Eight Flaps

Cut out the flap book around the outside border. Then, cut on the solid lines to create eight flaps. Apply glue to the back of the center section to attach it to a notebook page.

If desired, this template can be modified to create a six-flap or two four-flap books by cutting off the bottom row or two. You can also create a tall four-flap book by cutting off the flaps on the left side.

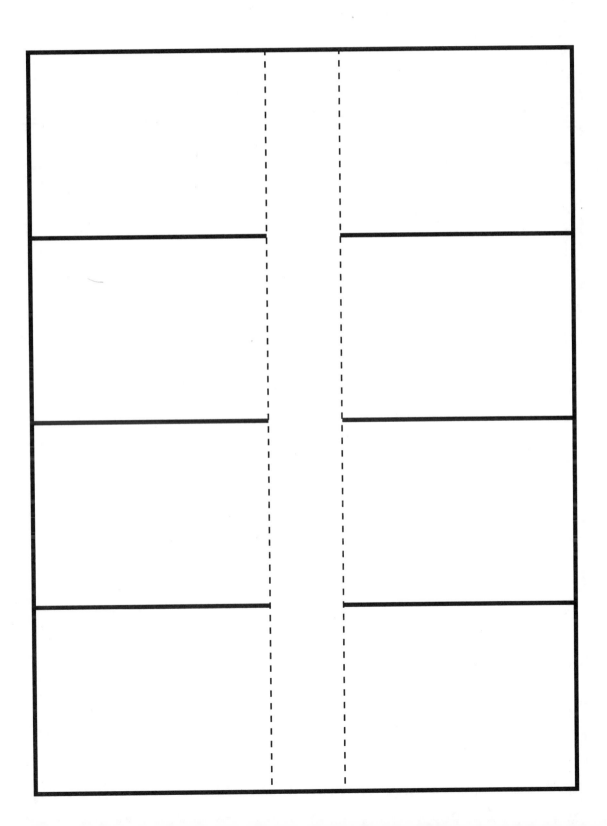

Flap Book—Twelve Flaps

Cut out the flap book around the outside border. Then, cut on the solid lines to create 12 flaps. Apply glue to the back of the center section to attach it to a notebook page.

If desired, this template can be modified to create smaller flap books by cutting off any number of rows from the bottom. You can also create a tall flap book by cutting off the flaps on the left side.

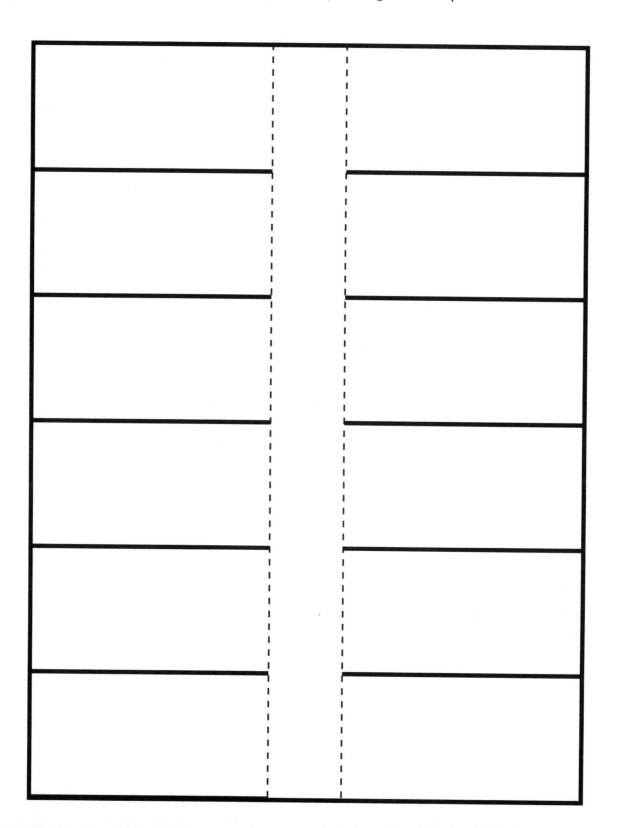

Shaped Flaps

Cut out each shaped flap. Apply glue to the back of the narrow section to attach it to a notebook page.

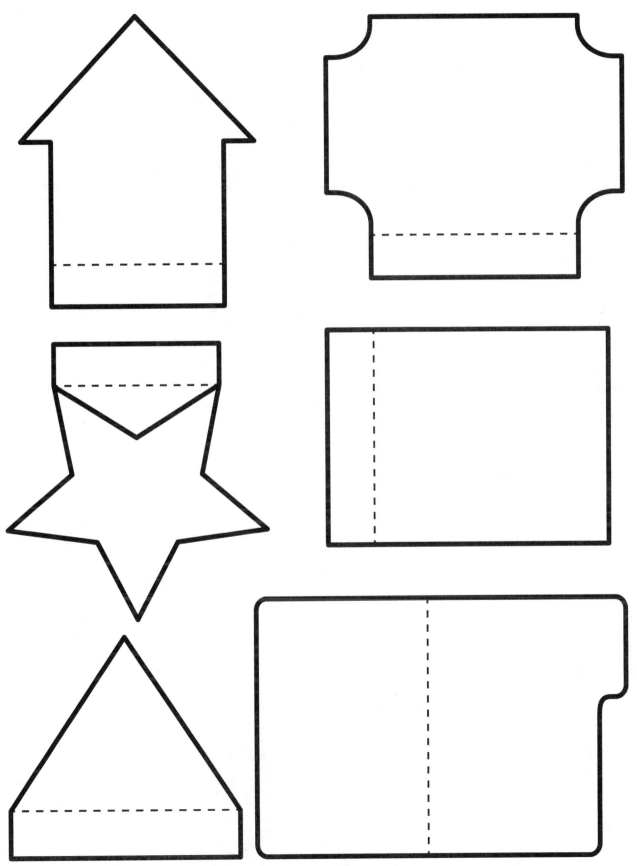

Shaped Flaps

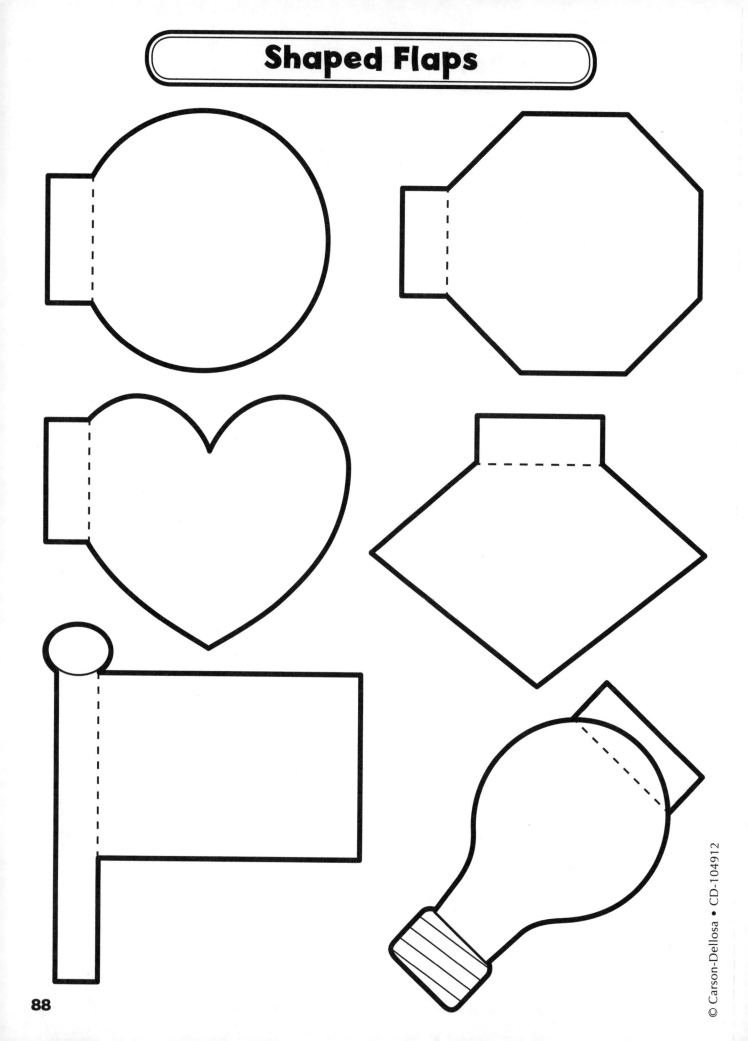

Interlocking Booklet

Cut out the booklet on the solid lines, including the short vertical lines on the top and bottom flaps. Then, fold the top and bottom flaps toward the center, interlocking them using the small vertical cuts. Apply glue to the back of the center panel to attach it to a notebook page.

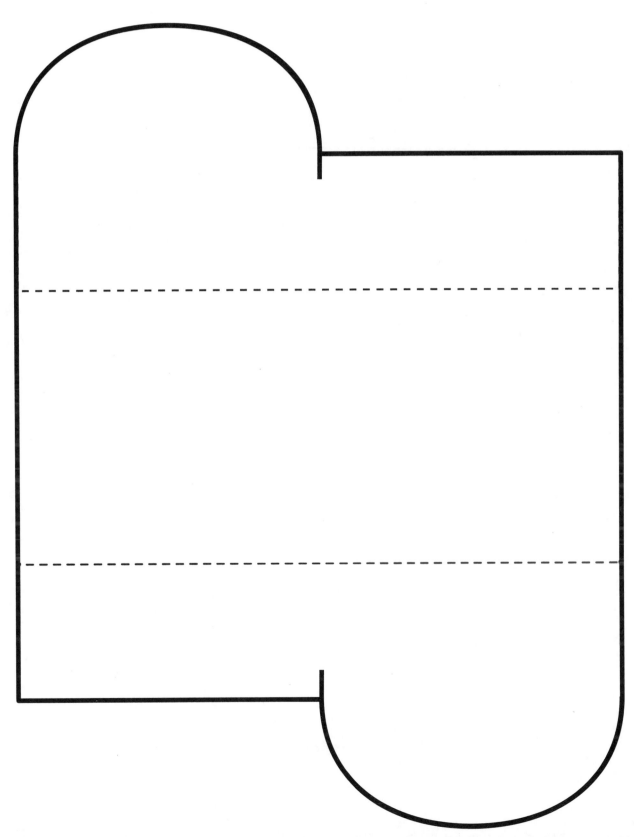

Four-Flap Petal Fold

Cut out the shape on the solid lines. Then, fold the flaps toward the center. Apply glue to the back of the center panel to attach it to a notebook page.

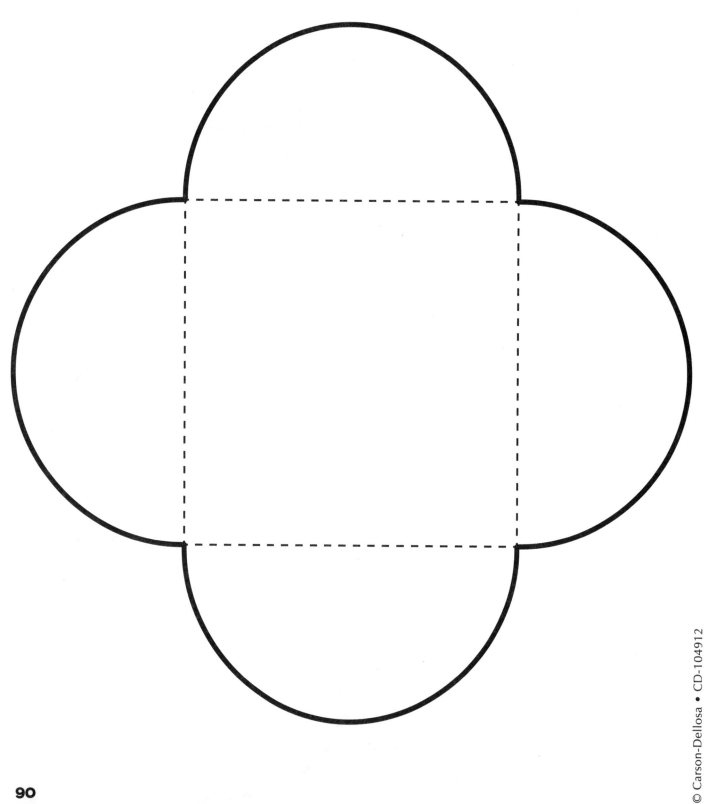

Six-Flap Petal Fold

Cut out the shape on the solid lines. Then, fold the flaps toward the center and back out. Apply glue to the back of the center panel to attach it to a notebook page.

Accordion Folds

Cut out the accordion pieces on the solid lines. Fold on the dashed lines, alternating the fold direction. Apply glue to the back of the last section to attach it to a notebook page.

You may modify the accordion books to have more or fewer pages by cutting off extra pages or by having students glue the first and last panels of two accordion books together.

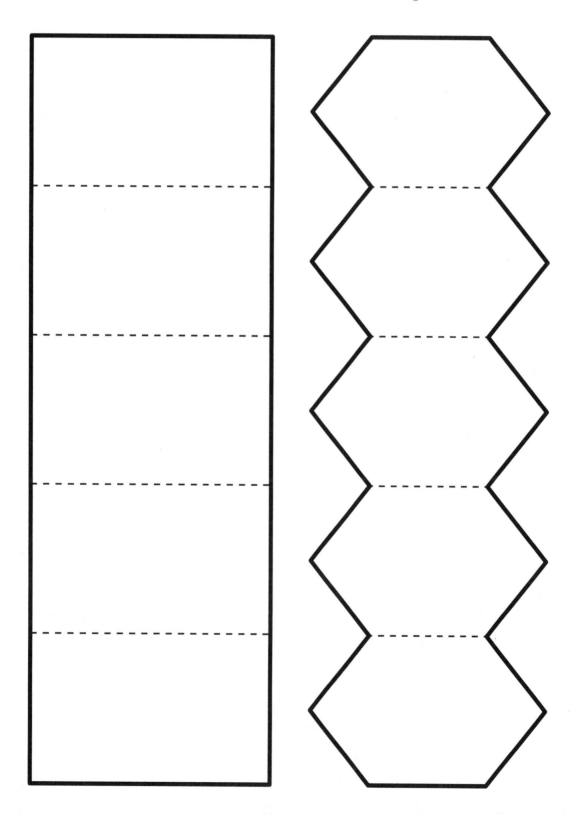

Accordion Folds

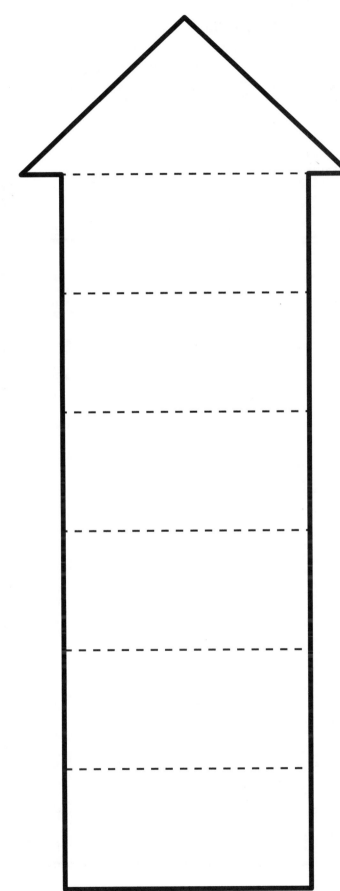

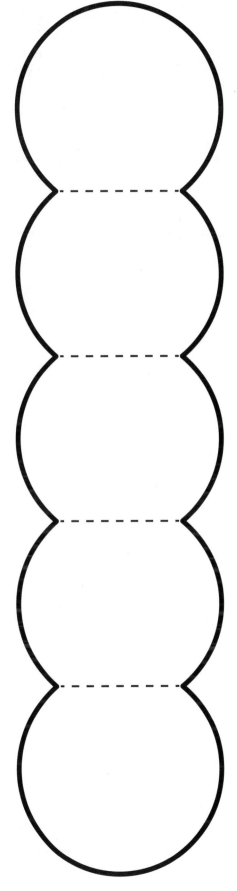

Clamshell Fold

Cut out the clamshell fold on the solid lines. Fold and unfold the piece on the three dashed lines. With the piece oriented so that the folds form an X with a horizontal line through it, pull the left and right sides together at the fold line. Then, keeping the sides touching, bring the top edge down to meet the bottom edge. You should be left with a triangular shape that unfolds into a square. Apply glue to the back of the triangle to attach the clamshell to a notebook page.

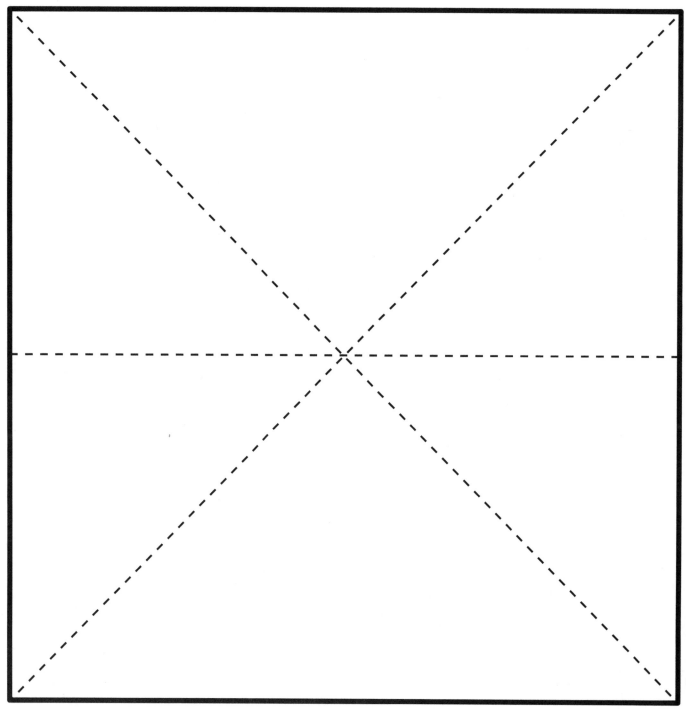

Puzzle Pieces

Cut out each puzzle along the solid lines to create a three- or four-piece puzzle. Apply glue to the back of each puzzle piece to attach it to a notebook page. Alternately, apply glue only to one edge of each piece to create flaps.

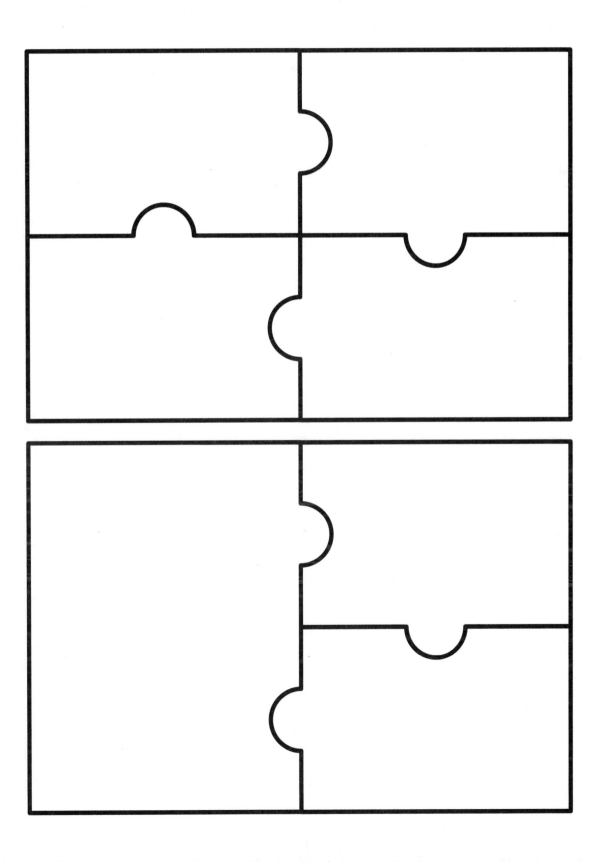

Flip Book

Cut out the two rectangular pieces on the solid lines. Fold each rectangle on the dashed lines. Fold the piece with the gray glue section so that it is inside the fold. Apply glue to the gray glue section and place the other folded rectangle on top so that the folds are nested and create a book with four cascading flaps. Make sure that the inside pages are facing up so that the edges of both pages are visible. Apply glue to the back of the book to attach it to a notebook page.

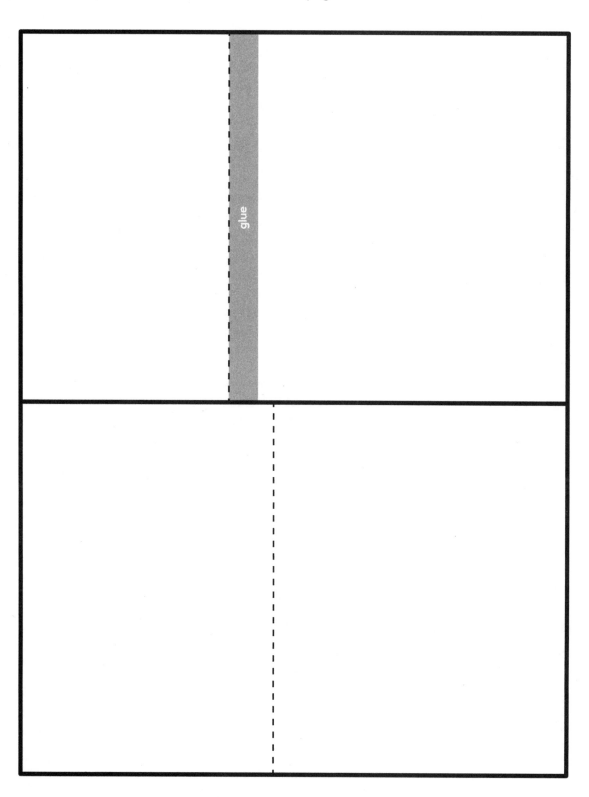

glue